WireStyle

denise peck

EDITOR OF STEP BY STEP WIRE JEWELRY

INTERWEAVE.
interweave.com

project photography joe coca
process photography jim lawson

art direction & cover design pamela norman
interior design stacy ebright

Interweave Press LLC
201 East Fourth Street
Loveland, CO 80537-5655 USA
interweave.com

Printed in China by Asia Pacific Offset

Library of Congress Cataloging-in-Publication Data

Peck, Denise.
  Wire style : 50 unique jewelry designs / Denise Peck, author.
     p. cm.
  Includes bibliographical references and index.
  ISBN 978-1-59668-070-8 (pbk.)
  1. Jewelry making. 2. Wire jewelry. I. Title.
  TT212.P425 2008
  739.27—dc22
                            2008003840

10 9 8 7 6

acknowledgments

First and foremost, my sincerest thanks to the artists who have contributed their designs and tutorials to the pages of this book. The jewelry world is filled with the most talented and generous people I've had the fortune to know. They never stop surprising me with their willingness to share their art.

Thanks to my colleagues, who make it a joy to come to work every day.

I am grateful to Linda Ligon and Tricia Waddell for believing from Day One that I should write a book.

And mostly, thanks to my husband, Paul, who has nothing but genuine and enthusiastic support for whatever endeavor I take on (not to mention the ability to fix whatever is ailing the computer).

– Denise Peck

contents

wire style

From the simplest to the most elaborate—that is the beauty of designing jewelry with wire. You can make a wedding band of a single ring of wire or a tiara ablaze with jewels. There is hardly a piece of jewelry that isn't made with some wire. Think about it: Every chain you see starts with wire. Every pierced earring has a post or hook made with wire. Every pin must have a pointed piece of wire to pierce your clothing. Wire is by far the most important element in the art of jewelry making.

It is also the most versatile. You can make designs in wire that are elegant, lush, lyrical, whimsical, austere, or even primitive. Designs can be evocative or literal. The material itself is available in a variety of shapes and sizes. It's made of silver, gold, aluminum, steel, brass, copper, and niobium. You can hammer it, bend it, twist it, fold it, coil it, file it, heat it, and even color it. But here's the best part: If you can hold a pair of pliers, you can make jewelry out of wire!

Maybe you're a beader ready to add to your jewelry-making repertoire. Maybe you want to make jewelry but haven't yet been lured by the magic of beads. Or maybe you've always wanted to be a metalsmith but were daunted by the time, space, and money required. Wire is the perfect answer. You can make wire jewelry with just a few very basic techniques. Every piece of jewelry in this book can be made using the techniques that are outlined and illustrated step by step in the first chapter. You'll also find a comprehensive reference guide for all the tools and materials you need for all the projects, plus a few more for when you're ready to expand your workshop.

The projects that follow are fifty brand-new designs by eight experienced jewelry makers. There is a wide array of styles in a selection of metals and colors—a smorgasbord of designs chosen for their originality and technique. If you learn how to make the designs in this book, you'll be able to make just about any piece of wire jewelry you desire. I hope this book not only introduces you to the wonderful world of wire but also awakens the design spirit that exists deep down in all of us jewelry lovers!

wire

One of the best things about working with wire is that it's such a forgiving medium. If you make a mistake, you can often restraighten the wire and begin again. Additionally, you can buy practice wire very inexpensively and create with impunity! Copper, brass, and colored craft wire are available in hardware and craft stores, and all of them can produce finished pieces every bit as beautiful as sterling silver and gold.

Wire comes in a large variety of metals, shapes, and sizes. The size or diameter of wire is known as the gauge. In the United States, the standard is Brown & Sharpe, also known as American Wire Gauge (AWG). The diameter of wire in inches or millimeters is translated into a numeral from 0 to 34, the higher the number, the thinner the wire. Most of the projects in this book use wire in 14-gauge through 24-gauge.

Wire also comes in a variety of shapes. You can buy round, half-round, and square wire. Round is most commonly used and easily available. Half-round has a flat side and is commonly used for ring shanks, and square wire has four flat sides. Both half-round and square wire must be ordered from a jeweler's supplier. In most cases, the choice of shape is purely aesthetic.

Additionally, a jeweler's supplier will offer wire in three hardnesses: dead soft, half hard, and full hard. Dead-soft wire is best if you're going to be manipulating it a lot because wire work-hardens as you work with it. Work-hardening stiffens the wire and makes it harder to bend. Eventually it can become so brittle that it can break with additional manipulation.

If you're weaving, coiling, or spiraling, you should work with dead-soft wire, as it's much easier on the hands. If you're making ear wires or not planning on working the wire too much, you can start with half-hard wire, which is already stiffer than dead-soft wire. There are no projects in this book that call for full-hard wire.

You can make jewelry out of both base-metal wire and precious-metal wire. The most common base-metal wire used in jewelry is copper, though aluminum, nickel silver, and brass are also available.

Sterling silver and gold wire are precious metals. The cost of gold wire is often prohibitive, so a common alternative is gold-filled wire, which is a base-metal wire covered with an outer layer of gold. Gold-filled wire is preferable to gold-plated wire because gold plating scratches and wears off easily.

As with the shape of the wire, the choice of metal is usually just a matter of personal preference.

gauge	round	half-round	square
2g	●	◗	■
3g	●	◗	■
4g	●	◗	■
6g	●	◗	■
7g	●	◗	■
8g	●	◗	■
9g	●	◗	■
10g	●	◗	■
11g	•	◗	■
12g	•	◗	■
13g	•	◗	■
14g	•	◗	■
16g	•	◗	■
18g	•	◗	■
19g	•	◗	■
20g	·	·	·
21g	·	·	·
22g	·	·	·
24g	·	·	·
26g	·	·	·

tools

Many wire jewelry projects require only two tools—pliers and cutters! Of course, there are plenty of supplemental tools to help simplify and enhance your work. Most wire workshops should have a set of good pliers and hammers, an anvil or steel bench block on which to hammer, some metal files for smoothing, and a supply of various-size mandrels around which you can coil wire. Mandrels can be anything from specialty tools for jewelry makers to pens and pencils, or even chopsticks!

general tools

1. flush cutters

These are also called side cutters because the cut is made to the side. They have pointed, angled jaws that allow very close cuts in tight places. One side of the jaws is almost flat, the other is concave. Always hold the flat side of the cutters against your work and the concave side against the waste. The flat side creates a nice flush end on your work. Flush cutters are sold with a maximum gauge-cutting capacity; be sure to use cutters that can accommodate the wire you're using.

2. mandrels

A mandrel is a spindle, rod, or bar around which you can bend metal or wire. They come in a variety of shapes and sizes. Some are made specifically for bracelets, some for rings, and some for making bezels. Almost anything can be used as a mandrel to shape wire, including wooden dowels and other pieces of wire. A Sharpie marker is a good example—it's the perfect shape for making French ear wires.

3. pin vise

Vises can hold a variety of tools, including blades and drill bits. They're perfectly suited for pinching and holding the end of a long piece of wire to enable you to turn smooth wire into twisted wire.

4. wire gauge

Also known as the Brown & Sharpe wire gauge, this tool looks a bit like a flat round gear. It measures the diameter of your wire and is an essential tool for wire jewelry making.

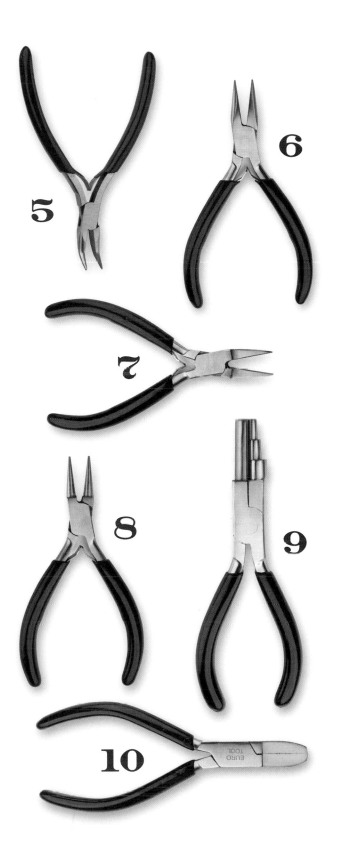

pliers

5. bent-nose pliers

Also called bent chain-nose pliers, these are similar to chain-nose pliers but have a bend at the tip that allows access to tight places for tasks such as tightening coils and tucking in ends. Two pairs used together are also helpful for opening and closing jump rings.

6. chain-nose pliers

The workhorse of wire tools, chain-nose pliers are like needle-nose pliers but without teeth that can mar your wire. They are used for grasping wire, opening and closing jump rings, and making sharp angled bends. It's a good idea to have at least two pairs in your workshop.

7. flat-nose pliers

Flat-nose pliers have broad, flat jaws and are good for making sharp bends in wire, grasping spirals, and holding components.

8. round-nose pliers

Another wireworker's necessity, round-nose pliers have pointed, graduated round jaws. They are used for making jump rings, simple loops, and curved bends in wire.

9. stepped forming pliers

Forming pliers come in different sizes and shapes. Stepped forming pliers have one chain-nose (or concave) jaw and one jaw of various size round barrels. They're perfect for wrapping loops of consistent size.

10. wire-straightening pliers

These are also called nylon-jaw pliers because the jaws are made of hard nylon. Pulling wire through the clamped jaws will straighten any bends or kinks. They can also be used to hold, bend, or shape wire without marring the metal. Keep in mind that every time you pull wire through straightening pliers, you're work-hardening it, making it more brittle and harder to manipulate.

hammering tools

11. awl

This common household tool comes in handy in a wire studio. A very sharp pointed tool, an awl usually has a wooden ball for a handle. Use it with a hammer to punch holes in flattened wire.

12. ball-peen hammer

Another staple in the studio, this hammer has one round domed head and one round flat head. The round head is used for making little dents for texture, while the flat head is used for flattening wire.

13. rawhide mallet

A hammer made of rawhide, this can be used on metal and wire without marring it. It's good for tapping wire into place or for hardening wire.

14. steel bench block

A bench block provides a small and portable hard surface on which to hammer wire. It's made of polished steel and is usually only ¾" (2 cm) thick and a few inches square. Use a bench block with a ball-peen hammer for flattening or texturing wire.

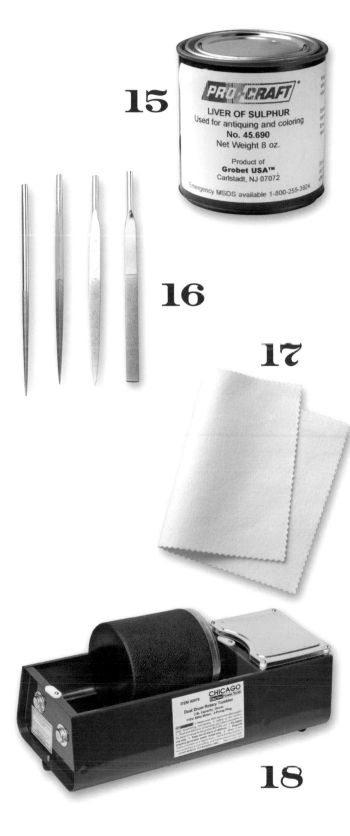

finishing tools

15. liver of sulfur

Liver of sulfur is a chemical traditionally used to darken silver wire. It comes in a liquid or solid chunk form and is used for oxidizing, or antiquing, wire. When a small amount is mixed with hot water, it will turn a piece of wire dipped in it from blue to gray to black. Very fine steel wool can be used to finish oxidized silver.

16. needle files

Needle files are made for smoothing sharp ends of metal and wire. They're small and fine and come in different shapes for different purposes. A flat needle file is often all you need for smoothing wire ends.

17. polishing cloth

Jewelry polishing cloths are infused with a polishing compound and can be used for cleaning wire, eliminating tarnish, and hardening wire; pulling wire through the cloth repeatedly will stiffen, or work-harden, it. Pro Polish is one of the most popular brands.

18. rotary tumbler

Often associated with rock tumbling, this same electrical piece of equipment can be used to polish wire and metal jewelry. The barrel must be filled with a tumbling medium such as stainless steel shot (available from jeweler's suppliers) and water. The tumbling action against the shot polishes the metal or wire to a high shine. The tumbling action also helps work-harden, or stiffen, the wire.

techniques

Similar to the tools, there are several basic techniques required to make wire jewelry. Over and above those, it's basically just tweaking a bit. If you can learn to make a nice round loop with your round-nose pliers, you're halfway there! Polishing and oxidizing can add a finishing touch.

The secret to fine wire jewelry is neatness. Ends should be neat and smooth or tucked out of sight. Coils should be tight and uniform, and loops should be round and centered.

basics

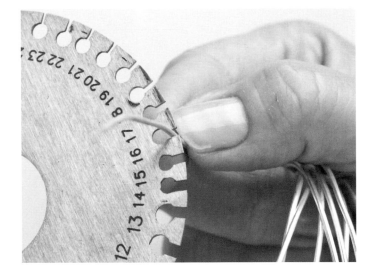

↑ using a wire gauge

Brown & Sharpe or AWG (American Wire Gauge) is the standard in the United States for measuring the diameter of wire. When you use a wire gauge, use the small slots around the edge of the gauge, not the round holes at the ends of the slots. Place the wire edge into a slot (Figure 1). If there's wiggle room, place it into the next smaller slot. When you reach a slot that it will not fit into, then the number at the end of the next larger slot is the gauge of your wire.

flush cutting

Flush cutters have two sides, a flat side and a concave side. When you cut wire, you want the end that remains on your working piece to be flat, or flush. To do this, make sure the flat side of the cutters is facing your working piece when you snip.

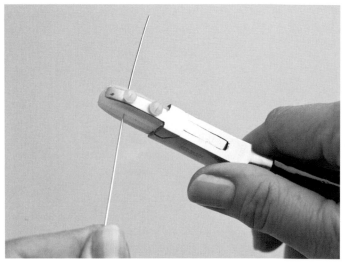

↑ straightening wire

Pulling a piece of wire through nylon-jaw pliers will straighten any bends in the wire. Grasp one end of the wire tightly in the nylon jaws and pull with your other hand (Figure 1). It may take two or three pulls through the pliers to straighten the wire completely. Be aware that the manipulation of wire in any pliers, including nylon-jaw pliers, will start the process of work-hardening the wire, which will eventually make it stiffer and harder to work with.

hammering

Always grasp the hammer firmly near the end of the handle. Do not "choke up" on the handle as you might a baseball bat. This assures you're using the weight of the head optimally and also keeps your hand from absorbing the shock of the impact.

loops

↓ simple loops

Grasp the end of the wire in round-nose pliers so you can just see the tip of the wire (Figure 1). Rotate the pliers fully until you've made a complete loop (Figure 2). Remove the pliers. Reinsert the tip of the pliers to grasp the wire directly across from the opening of the loop. Make a sharp 45° bend across from the opening (Figure 3), centering the loop over the length of the wire like a lollipop (Figure 4).

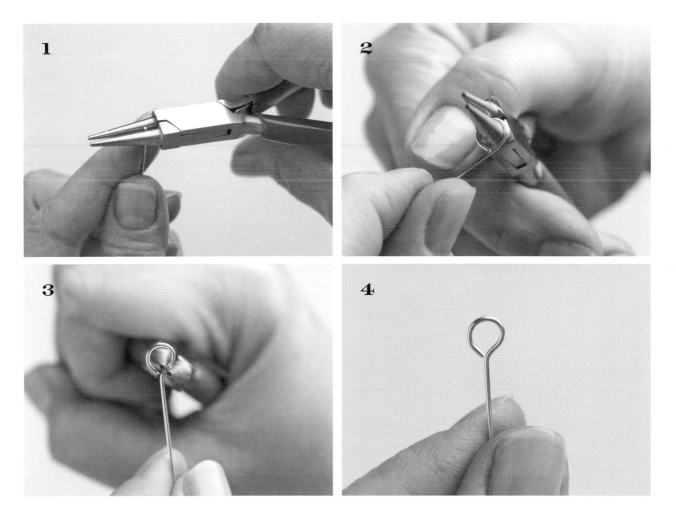

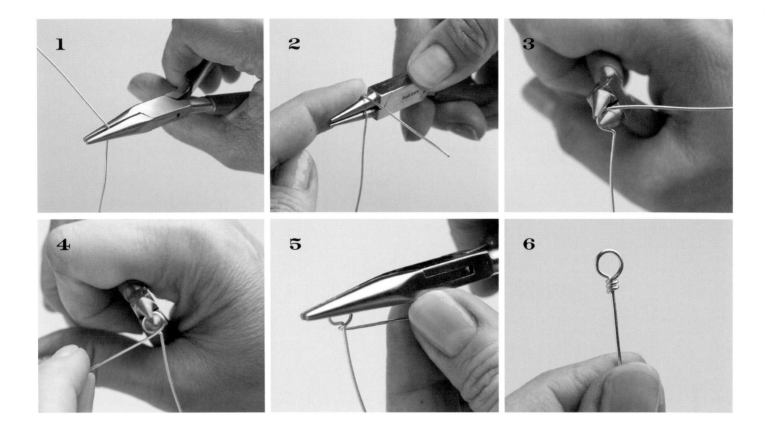

loops

↑ wrapped loops

Grasp the wire about 2" (5 cm) from the end with chain-nose pliers. Using your fingers, bend the wire flat against the pliers to 90° (Figure 1). With round-nose pliers, grasp the wire right at the bend you just made, holding the pliers perpendicular to the tabletop. Pull the wire up and over the top of the round-nose pliers (Figure 2). Pull the pliers out and put the lower jaw back into the loop you just made (Figure 3). Continue pulling the wire around the bottom jaw of the pliers into a full round loop (Figure 4). With your fingers or chain-nose pliers, wrap the wire around the neck of the lower wire two or three times (Figures 5 and 6).

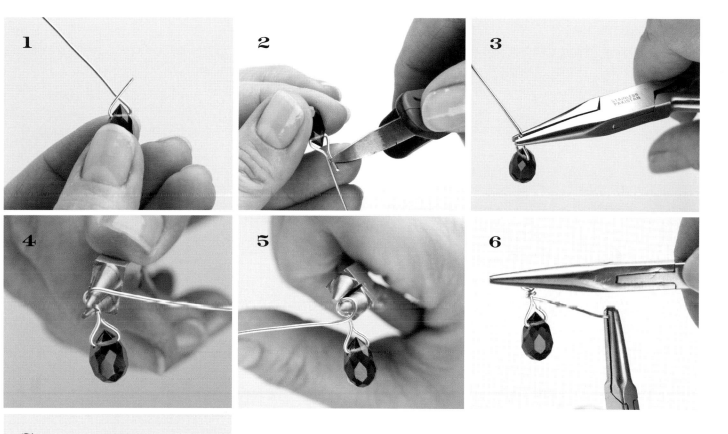

loops
↑ briolette loops

For top-drilled stones, insert a wire through the hole and bend up both sides so that they cross over the top of the stone (Figure 1). (You will only need a short length on one side.) Make a bend in each of the wires so they point straight up off the top of the stone. With flush cutters, trim the short wire so that it's no longer than ⅛" (3 mm) (Figure 2). Pinch the two wires together with chain-nose pliers and bend the longer wire over the top of the shorter wire to 90° (Figure 3). Make a wrapped loop by switching to round-nose pliers and pulling the long wire up and over the round jaw (Figures 4 and 5). Wrap the neck of the two wires together two or three times to secure (Figures 6 and 7).

coils and spirals

coiling →

Coils can be made on any round mandrel, including another piece of wire. Hold one end of the wire tightly against the mandrel with your thumb and coil the length up the mandrel. Be sure to wrap snugly and keep the coils right next to one another (Figure 1). Flush cut both ends (Figure 2). Slide the coil off the mandrel.

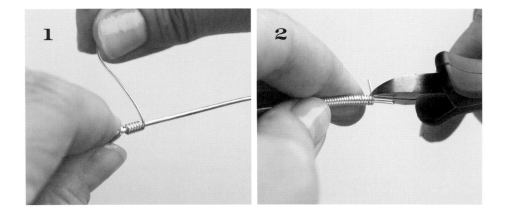

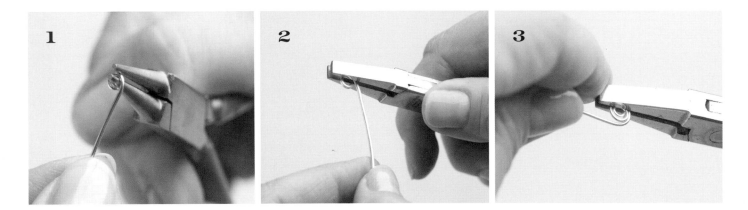

↑ spiraling

Make a very small loop with round-nose pliers (Figure 1). Grasp the loop in flat-nose pliers and use the thumb of your other hand to push the wire around the loop (Figure 2). Continue to move the spiral around in the jaws of the flat-nose pliers to enable you to enlarge the coil (Figure 3).

jump rings

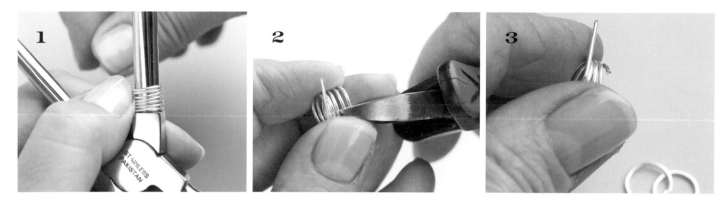

↑ making jump rings

Coil wire snugly around a mandrel (Figure 1). Each single coil will make one jump ring. Remove the mandrel. Using flush cutters, cut through all the rings at the same spot along the length of the coil, snipping one or two at a time (Figure 2). They will fall away and each ring will be slightly open (Figure 3). The jump rings you make will have the inner diameter (ID) of the mandrel you used to make them.

When purchasing jump rings, note that some vendors sell them by inner diameter measurements and some vendors sell them by outer diameter measurements. The difference is minuscule and only essential if you're working on a complex chain maille design.

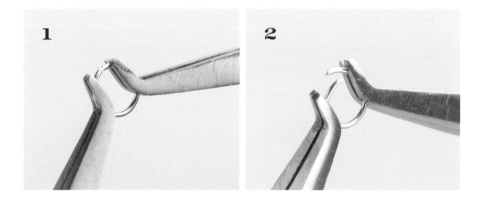

↑ opening and closing jump rings

Always use two chain-nose or bent-nose pliers to open and close jump rings. Grasp the ring on each side of the opening with pliers (Figure 1). Gently push one side away from you while pulling the other side toward you, so the ring opens from side to side (Figure 2). To close, reverse the directions of your hands.

links

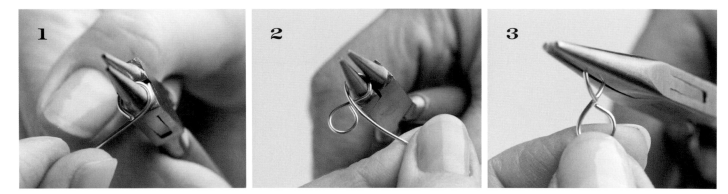

hooks

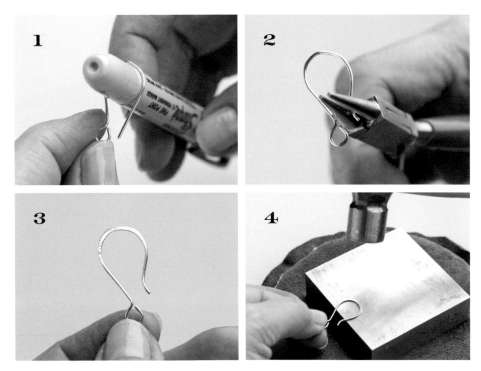

↑ figure-eight links

Make a loop on one end of the wire with round-nose pliers (Figure 1). Remove the pliers and grasp the wire just below the loop you just made. Pull the wire around the jaw of the pliers in the opposite direction of the first loop (Figure 2). Make sure you work at the same point on the jaw that you used to make the first loop so that the loops are the same size. Flush cut the end. Optional: Hold one loop with your fingers, grasp the other loop with chain-nose pliers, and twist a quarter turn so that the loops sit perpendicular to each other (Figure 3).

← simple hooks

Make a simple loop on the end of the wire with round-nose pliers. Hold a Sharpie marker against the wire above the loop and bend the wire over the marker and down parallel to the loop (Figure 1). Flush cut the long wire across from the loop. With round-nose pliers, make a small bend outward at the end of the hook (Figure 2). Flatten the curve of the hook with a ball-peen hammer to work-harden and strengthen the hook (Figures 3 and 4).

hooks

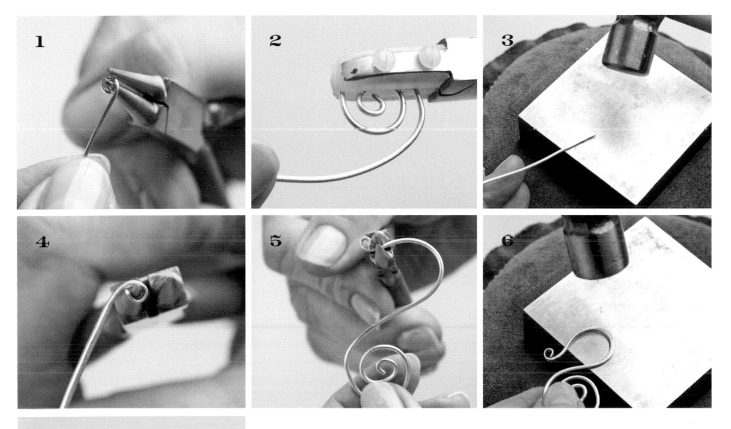

↑ spiral hooks

This clasp can be made with a tight spiral or a loose, open spiral. Both begin with a small loop made with round-nose pliers (Figure 1). With flat-nose or nylon-jaw pliers, make a spiral (Figure 2). Leave about 2" (5 cm) wire beyond the spiral, and at the other end of the wire flatten ¼" (6 mm) with a ball-peen hammer (Figure 3). Make a very small loop in the same direction as the spiral (Figure 4). Using pliers or your fingers, bend the length back away from the small loop and into a hook (Figure 5). Flatten the curve of the hook with a ball-peen hammer to work-harden and strengthen the hook (Figures 6 and 7).

hooks

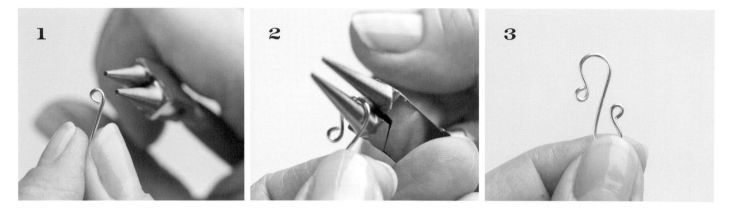

↑ s-hooks

This clasp can be made in any size, depending on the length of wire you start with. With round-nose pliers, make a small loop on each end, going in opposite directions (Figure 1). Grasp one side with round-nose pliers just above the loop and bend the wire back over the pliers away from the loop (Figure 2). Turn the wire over and repeat in the opposite direction on the other end (Figure 3).

ear wires

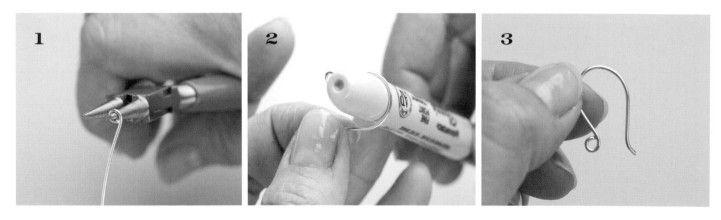

↑ ear wires

With round-nose pliers, make a small loop on the end of a 1½" (3.8 cm) length of wire (Figure 1). Hold the loop against a Sharpie marker and bend the wire over the marker away from the loop (Figure 2). With round-nose pliers, make a small bend outward at the end of the wire (Figure 3).

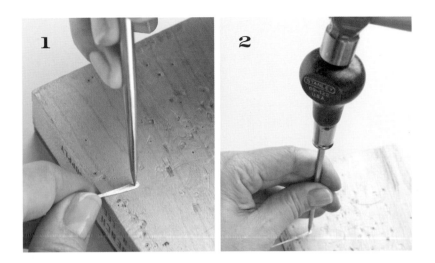

other techniques

← piercing

If wire has been flattened, you can pierce it with an awl to make a hole for connecting other elements, such as ear wires. It's best to work on a scrap piece of wood. Take a sharp awl and position it where you want the hole. Push firmly to make an impression—a starter spot (Figure 1). Then place the point of the awl in the impression and strike the top sharply with a hammer (Figure 2).

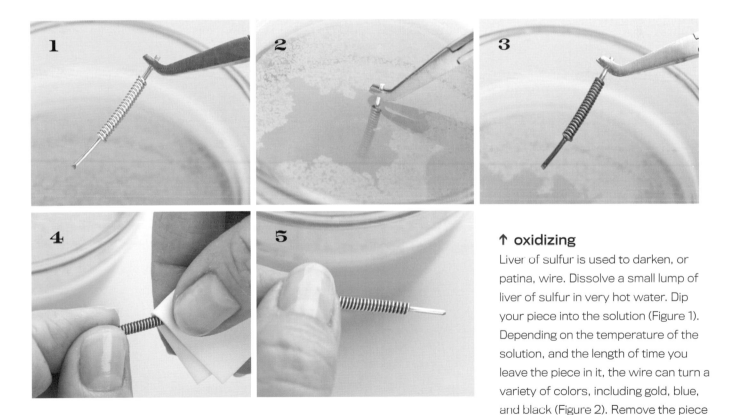

↑ oxidizing

Liver of sulfur is used to darken, or patina, wire. Dissolve a small lump of liver of sulfur in very hot water. Dip your piece into the solution (Figure 1). Depending on the temperature of the solution, and the length of time you leave the piece in it, the wire can turn a variety of colors, including gold, blue, and black (Figure 2). Remove the piece when it reaches the desired color (Figure 3). Dry and polish it lightly to remove some of the patina (Figure 4), but leave the dark color in the recesses of the piece (Figure 5).

projects

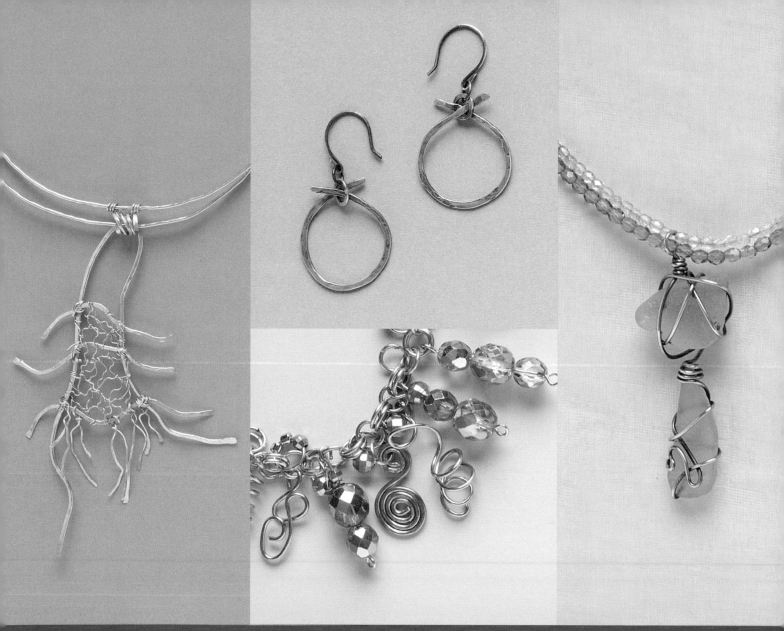

It can be fun to infuse some color into your wire projects. That's easily done when you work with anodized aluminum jump rings, which are available in an array of colors, sizes, and gauges.

daisy chain bracelet

denise peck

TECHNIQUES USED
opening and closing jump rings, page 22
simple hooks, page 20

MATERIALS
31 assorted-color anodized aluminum 14-gauge
⁷⁄₁₆" (1.1cm) ID jump rings
7 single-color anodized aluminum 18-gauge
⁵⁄₁₆" (8mm) ID jump rings

TOOLS
2 chain-nose pliers

FINISHED SIZE
7¾" (19.5 cm)

1. Separate the 14g jump rings into piles of 3 same-color rings. Each daisy is made up of 3 jump rings.

2. From the first pile, open 1 jump ring, pass through 1 ring, and close ring. Open the third ring and thread it through the "eye" where the 2 previous rings are joined, being sure to pass through both. Repeat for a total of 8 daisies.

3. Open one 18g jump ring and use it to connect 2 daisies, passing through all 3 rings of both daisies, and close. Repeat to join all 8 daisies.

4. Attach 3 remaining 14g jump rings in a chain and attach one end to the last daisy on one side of the bracelet. Repeat at the other end.

5. Open the last 14g jump ring, bend it into a simple hook, and attach it to one end of the bracelet.

all wrapped up

sandra lupo

Not every stone is drilled into a bead. Use this wrapping technique to capture a beautiful rock specimen for a focal pendant, purchased or found. You can use this same technique on a favorite seashell.

TECHNIQUES USED

simple loops, page 15
making jump rings, page 19
simple hooks, page 20

MATERIALS

3' (91.5 cm) of sterling silver 12-gauge dead-soft half-round wire
4" (10 cm) of sterling silver 20-gauge half-hard round wire
1 gem silica 2 x 1 x ⅞" (50mm x 27mm x 22mm) rock
2 turquoise 1 x 2mm African opal cylinder beads
12" (30.5 cm) of sterling silver rolo chain, cut in half
5" (12.5 cm) of sterling silver varying link chain, cut in half

TOOLS

Flush cutters
Flat-nose pliers
Chain-nose pliers

FINISHED SIZE

20¾" (52.5 cm)

1. Cut 24" (61 cm) of 12g half-round wire. Beginning at the middle of the length, press the flat side of the wire against the middle of one side of the rock and begin to wrap.

2. As you near a surface edge, use the flat-nose pliers to form a sharp angle. At the next edge, angle the wire with the pliers once again. Be careful of hugging the rock too closely at the edge, as stones such as opal and silica might chip against the heavy wire. It is best to allow the angles to form near and past but not right at the surface edge.

3. Continue to wrap and create sharp angles. If the end of the rock is tapered, make closer wraps to create a spiral effect. Wrap until you come to the end of the rock.

4. Repeat Steps 2 and 3 with the other half of the wire, working toward the other end of the rock.

5. Use chain-nose pliers to lift the last angled spiral into a squared-off simple loop on each end of the stone.

6. Cut two 1½" (3.8 cm) lengths of 12g half-round wire and wrap each cylinder bead.

7. Cut two 2" (5 cm) lengths of 20g round wire. Thread each cylinder bead onto a length of 20g round sterling wire and make a simple loop on each end.

8. Connect a piece of varying link chain to one end of the wrapped rock by opening the simple loop and connect the other end to a cylinder bead; repeat at the other end of the rock with the other length of chain and the other cylinder bead. Connect one piece of rolo chain to the remaining end of each cylinder bead.

9. Use 2" (5 cm) of half-round 12g wire to make a simple hook clasp to finish. Attach to the remaining end of one length of rolo chain. Use 1" (2.5 cm) of half-round 12g wire to form a 7mm jump ring. Attach to the remaining end of the other length of rolo chain.

Elongated eye pins form the links in this wild necklace, and a simple 90° bend holds the disc beads in place. Let loose and have fun with this random twisted-wire design.

definitely looped
kerry bogert

TECHNIQUES USED
simple loops, page 15
wrapped loops, page 16
simple hooks, page 20
opening and closing jump rings, page 19

MATERIALS
8' (2.4 m) of sterling silver 18-gauge dead-soft wire
12–14 assorted multicolored 15–20mm lampworked coins
   with $\frac{1}{16}$" (2mm) holes
1 sterling silver 6mm jump ring

TOOLS
Flush cutters
Round-nose pliers
$\frac{1}{8}$" (3 mm) steel mandrel
Rotary tumbler
Stainless steel shot

FINISHED SIZE
18" (45.5 cm)

1. Eye pins: Cut ten to twelve 8" (20.5 cm) lengths of wire. Using round-nose pliers, make a small simple loop on the end of each cut piece of wire to form an eye pin. This loop will hold the disc beads in place.

2. For the first link, slide 1 bead onto 1 eye pin and make a 90° bend in the wire behind the bead to lock it against the small loop.

3. Starting right behind the bead, randomly wrap the remaining length of wire around the mandrel. This creates the "loopy" winds of the link. At the end of the loopy link, make a wrapped loop.

4. For the next link, string 1 bead and the wire-wrapped loop of the first link onto 1 eye pin. Make a 90° bend, locking both the bead and the link against the small loop. Randomly wrap the long length of wire around the mandrel as in Step 3 and close with a wrapped loop. Repeat for desired length of necklace, making the wrapped loop on the last link larger than the rest to act as the eye for the clasp.

5. Make a simple hook clasp and attach it to the other end with the jump ring.

6. Tumble the finished piece in a rotary tumbler with stainless steel shot for about 1½ hours to work-harden the links.

Make a statement with this large S-curve pendant. Flattened curves give a handwrought effect, and the wrapped wire adds a professional touch. Accented by silver charms, this pendant is fun to make and fun to wear.

"s" is for silver

tamara C. honaman

TECHNIQUES USED
coiling, page 18
hammering, page 15
simple loops, page 15
s hooks, page 22
opening and closing jump rings, page 19
wrapped loops, page 16

MATERIALS
12" (30.5 cm) of sterling silver 20-gauge
   dead-soft twisted wire
7" (18 cm) of sterling silver 14-gauge half-hard wire
1 20mm lampworked bead
2 silver charms
2 Bali silver 12mm disc spacers
2 sterling silver 5mm disc spacers
1 sterling silver 20-gauge head pin
3 sterling silver 18-gauge 3mm ID jump rings
1 sterling silver 16-gauge 8mm ID jump ring
1 silk 36" (91.5 cm) handstitched "fairy" ribbon

TOOLS
5" (12.5 cm) of copper 14-gauge wire (to use for mandrel)
Round-nose pliers
Chain-nose pliers
Ball-peen hammer
Steel bench block
Large Sharpie marker or wooden dowel

FINISHED SIZE
3½" (9 cm)

1. Wrap the twisted wire around the 14g copper wire to create a 1¾" (4.5 cm) coil. Remove the coil from the copper wire and center it on the sterling silver 14g wire.

2. Place one end of the sterling silver 14g wire on the steel bench block and hammer ½" (1.3 cm). Repeat at the other end.

3. Using the round-nose pliers, make a simple loop on each end of the 14g silver wire so that the loops are facing opposite directions.

4. Place the barrel of the marker or dowel on the 14g silver wire below one of the simple loops. Bend the wire around the marker or dowel to create the first bend in the S as though making an S-hook.

5. Place the barrel of the marker or dowel on the other side of the wire below the simple loop and bend the wire to form the other half of the S. The simple loops should meet near the middle.

6. Place the curve of one half of the S onto the bench block and hammer to flatten the wire. Repeat for the other half.

7. Open one 3mm jump ring, add the loop of 1 charm, and close the jump ring. Repeat for the other charm. Add a second 3mm jump ring to one of the charms.

8. Place 1 disc spacer, 1 Bali silver spacer, the lampworked bead, 1 Bali silver spacer, 1 disc spacer, and the jump rings of both charms on the head pin. Make a wrapped loop around the bottom of the S.

9. Open the 8mm jump ring, add the top loop of the S, and close the jump ring. String the jump ring onto the ribbon.

This bracelet makes a common design element, a coiled spiral hook, into a focal piece. When combining wire with leather or other cording materials, oxidize the wire first to avoid dipping the leather into liver of sulfur solution.

i'm hooked

ronna sarvas weltman

MATERIALS

12" (30.5 cm) of sterling silver 14-gauge dead-soft
  wire
12" (30.5 cm) of oxidized sterling silver 22-gauge
  dead-soft wire
10" (25.5 cm) of colored leather cord

TOOLS

Flush cutters
Round-nose pliers
Chain-nose pliers
Ball-peen hammer
Steel bench block
Liver of sulfur
Polishing cloth

FINISHED SIZE

6½" (16.5 cm)

1. Use 14g wire to make a large spiral hook about the width of your wrist. Use the ball-peen hammer to texture it.

2. Bend the clasp into a slightly curved shape that mimics the curve of your wrist so it will sit gracefully.

3. Oxidize and polish the clasp.

4. To estimate the length of leather cord needed, wrap the leather once around your wrist and add 4" (10 cm). Cut with flush cutters.

5. Fold the leather in half. Using the oxidized 22g wire, lash the leather together by coiling wire about ten times around both pieces of leather about ½" (1.3 cm) from the fold, leaving a center loop.

6. Slip the loop onto the large coiled side of the clasp. Lay the clasp on your wrist and fold back the leather ends to form a loop around the other side of the clasp.

7. Hold onto the loop as you remove the bracelet from your wrist. Use the 22g wire to lash all four pieces of leather together, forming a coil on that side. Trim leather ends.

This charm necklace has so many possibilities—use smaller beads for a more delicate look, nuggets for a chunkier look, or smaller pearls for an elegant look. The bead-and-wire dangles show off lovely spirals and wrapped loops.

grape clusters
jodi l. bombardier

TECHNIQUES USED
wrapped loops, page 16
spiraling, page 18
opening and closing jump rings, page 19
spiral hooks, page 22

MATERIALS
24' (7.3 m) of sterling silver 24-gauge half-hard wire
6¼" (16 cm) of sterling silver 16-gauge dead-soft wire
76 purple 8mm freshwater pearls
20 fluorite 8mm barrel beads
8 sterling silver 18-gauge 6mm jump rings
8" (20.5 cm) of sterling silver chain, cut into one 3½" (9 cm) segment and one 4½" (11.5 cm) segment
48 Bali silver daisy spacers

TOOLS
Flush cutters
Round-nose pliers
Chain-nose pliers

FINISHED SIZE
16" (40.5 cm)

1. Cut forty-seven 6" (15 cm) pieces of 24g wire.

2. Make a wrapped loop at one end of one wire. String 1 pearl, 1 spacer, and 1 pearl. Make another wrapped loop. Repeat for a total of 4 links.

3. Make a wrapped loop at one end of one wire. String 1 fluorite bead, 1 spacer, and 1 pearl. Make another wrapped loop. Repeat for a total of 3 links.

4. Make a small spiral at one end of one wire. Make a 90° bend at the top of the spiral. String 1 pearl, 1 spacer, and 1 pearl. Make another wrapped loop. Repeat for a total of 24 pearl charms.

5. Make a small spiral at one end of one wire. Make a 90° bend at the top of the spiral. String 1 fluorite bead, 1 spacer, and 1 pearl. Make another wrapped loop. Repeat for a total of 16 charms.

6. Assembly: Open 1 jump ring. Slip onto the jump ring the 4½" (11.5 cm) segment of chain, 1 fluorite/pearl spiral, 1 pearl/pearl spiral, 1 pearl/pearl link, 1 pearl/pearl spiral, 1 fluorite/pearl spiral, and 1 pearl/pearl spiral, being careful to keep them in order. Close the jump ring.

7. Open 1 jump ring and slip it onto the wrapped loop at the other end of the pearl/pearl link added in Step 6. Add 1 pearl/pearl spiral, 1 fluorite/pearl spiral, 1 pearl/pearl spiral, 1 fluorite/pearl link, 1 fluorite/pearl spiral, and 1 pearl/pearl spiral. Close the jump ring.

8. Repeat Steps 6 and 7 three times. Repeat Step 6. On the last link, add the 3½" (9 cm) segment of chain. Make one more fluorite/pearl spiral and attach it to the last link of chain.

9. Clasp: Make a spiral hook and attach it to the last link on the other length of chain.

A series of beads stacked on head pins forms a tight circle adorning these lampworked bead earrings. The head pins are hidden, which makes the beads appear to float above the beautiful focal beads.

glass nests

tamara l. honaman

TECHNIQUES USED
simple loops, page 15
wrapped loops, page 16

MATERIALS
2 lampworked 16mm beads
6 bronze 3mm cultured freshwater pearls
6 erinite 6mm crystal rondelles
2 apatite 8mm rondelles
4 Bali silver 5mm spacer beads
2 sterling silver 18-gauge head pins
12 sterling silver 24-gauge head pins
1 pair of leverback ear wires

TOOLS
Round-nose pliers
Bent-nose pliers

FINISHED SIZE
1½" (3.8 cm)

1. String 1 pearl on one 24g head pin and make a simple loop. Repeat to make 6 pearl dangles.

2. String 1 Swarovski rondelle bead on one 24g head pin and make a simple loop. Repeat to make 6 crystal dangles.

3. String 1 spacer and 1 lampworked bead on one 18g head pin. Alternating pearls and crystals, string 3 pearl dangles and 3 crystal dangles. String 1 rondelle and 1 spacer. Make a wrapped loop to secure all beads. Repeat with remaining beads, dangles, and head pin.

4. Using the bent-nose pliers, open the loop on the bottom of 1 ear wire, string 1 wrapped loop, and close the loop on the ear wire. Repeat for second earring.

These earrings are fast, easy, and unusual!
Make several pairs with different beads on the ends
to vary the look—they'll all be interesting and fun to wear.

winding vines
denise peck

MATERIALS
12" (30.5 cm) of sterling silver 20-gauge half-hard wire
2 stone 17 x 22mm top-drilled leaves

TOOLS
Nylon-jaw straightening pliers
Flush cutters
Round-nose pliers
Flat-nose pliers
Pencil or ring mandrel

FINISHED SIZE
2½" (6.5 cm)

1. Pass the 20g wire through the straightening pliers several times to stiffen it. Cut the wire in half.

2. Make a sharp bend 2¼" (5.5 cm) from the end of each wire and curve it slightly with your fingers to make the ear wire.

3. Wind the other end of each wire around the pencil or ring mandrel, leaving the end straight and long enough to accommodate the bead.

4. String the bead on the straight end of the wire. Make a small simple loop with the round-nose pliers to anchor the bead.

TECHNIQUES USED
straightening wire, page 14
coiling, page 18
simple loops, page 15

This unusual chain requires jump rings in two different sizes and gauges, which gives it a fluid side-to-side movement. As the smaller links creep along the edges, you will see where it gets its name!

centipede
howard siegel

TECHNIQUES USED

making jump rings, page 19
opening and closing jump rings, page 19

MATERIALS

10' (3 m) of sterling silver 16-gauge dead-soft wire
8' (2.4 m) of sterling silver 18-gauge dead-soft wire
1 sterling silver 13mm lobster clasp

TOOLS

8mm mandrel
3mm mandrel
Flush cutters
2 chain-nose pliers
1 twist tie (the type used to close grocery bags)
Rotary tumbler
Stainless steel shot

FINISHED SIZE

29¼" (74.5 cm)

1. Wind the 16g silver wire into coils on the 8mm mandrel, making about fifty turns at a time so they're not too difficult to cut. Repeat to make 98 jump rings.

2. Wind the 18g silver wire into coils on the 3mm mandrel, making about fifty turns at a time so they're not too difficult to cut. Repeat to make 196 jump rings.

3. Carefully close all of the large rings using 2 chain-nose pliers.

4. Open all the small rings about 60°.

5. Place the twist tie through one of the large rings and twist closed. This is the starter ring. Place a second large ring on top of and about halfway across the starter ring. The rings form an "eye" where they overlap. Hold the 2 large rings in this position with the thumb and forefinger.

6. With chain-nose pliers, place a small ring through the "eye" at one side of the 2 large rings. Close the ring using 2 chain-nose pliers. Place a second small ring through the "eye" on the opposite side from the first small ring and close.

7. Place a third large ring on top of and about halfway across the second large ring. Add the 2 small rings as in Step 6.

8. Continue adding large and small rings in this same manner until the chain measures 28" (71 cm).

9. Remove the twist tie from the starting end of the chain. Open the last jump ring, add the lobster clasp, and close the jump ring.

10. Tumble the chain for about an hour with stainless steel shot and burnishing compound to polish and remove any rough burrs. Remove the chain from the tumbler, rinse in clean running water, and dry with a terry towel.

Copper, brass, and silver wires create the look of tricolor gold
without the high price tag in this simple chain maille bracelet.
Fashioning your own jump rings makes it even more economical.

3 x 3

linda gettings

MATERIALS
6' (1.8 m) of copper 20-gauge wire
4' (1.2 m) of sterling silver 20-gauge wire
4' (1.2 m) of brass 20-gauge wire
3" (7.5 cm) of brass 18-gauge wire

TOOLS
6mm and 8mm dowels
Flush cutters
Round-nose pliers
2 chain-nose pliers

FINISHED SIZE
7" (18 cm)

1. Using the 8mm dowel, make 52 jump rings in each of the
20g wires, keeping same-colored rings together.

2. Use the chain-nose pliers to close 2 copper rings.
Attach 2 open copper rings and close; repeat until the
chain is long enough to fit your wrist. In the same way,
make double-link chains in silver and brass.

3. Make 104 copper jump rings using the 6mm dowel.

4. Lay the three lengths of chain out flat. Use two 6mm
jump rings to connect each link of the brass chain to each
link of the silver chain, being sure to pass through both
rings in each link. Repeat to join each link of the copper
chain to each link of the silver chain.

5. With the 18g wire, make a simple hook and one 8mm
jump ring and attach them through all 6 rings at each end
of the chain.

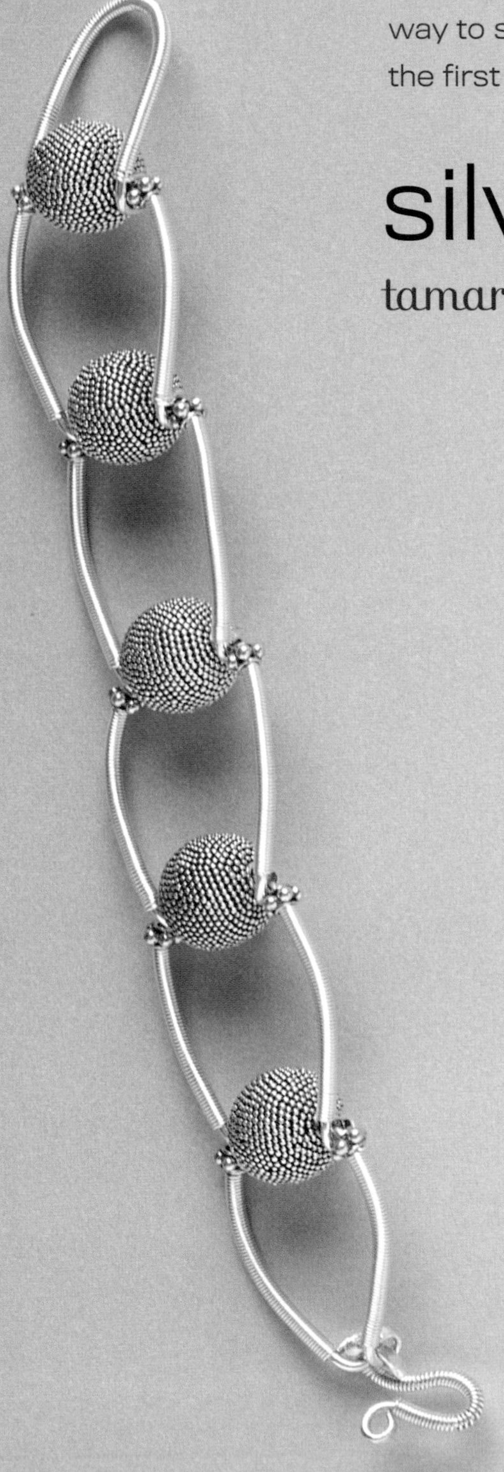

Every link of this cuff is made with coiled wire. It's a beautiful way to set off the intricate Bali beads. The clasp connects to the first link for a simple but elegant closure.

silver springs

tamara l. honaman

TECHNIQUES USED

coiling, page 18

hammering, page 15

simple loops, page 15

simple hooks, page 20

MATERIALS

24" (61 cm) of sterling silver 16-gauge half-hard wire
10' (3 m) of sterling silver 24-gauge dead-soft wire
5 Bali silver 13mm beads
10 Bali silver 5mm spacers

TOOLS

18" (45.5 cm) of copper 16-gauge wire (to use as a
    mandrel)
Flush cutters
Heavy-duty wire cutters (able to cut 16-gauge wire)
Round-nose pliers
Chain-nose pliers
Flat-nose pliers
Ball-peen hammer
Steel bench block

FINISHED SIZE

7¼" (18.5 cm)

1. Coil the 24g silver wire around the 16g copper wire until
the coil is about 14" (35.5 cm) long. 8½" (21.5 cm) of 24g
wire will produce 1" (2.5 cm) of 24g coil. Remove the coil
from the 16g wire. Cut the coil into one 2" (5 cm) length
and eleven 1" (2.5 cm) lengths.

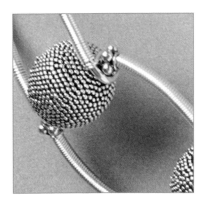

2. Cut the 16g silver
wire into five 4" (10 cm)
lengths: one 3" (7.5 cm)
length; one 2" (5 cm)
length; and one 1¼" (3.2
cm) length.

3. Place the end of the
3" (7.5 cm) length of
16g silver wire onto the
bench block. Hammer ¼" (6 mm) of one end. Grip the end
of the flattened section with the round-nose pliers and
make a simple loop. String the 2" (5 cm) coil onto the open
end. Hammer ¼" (6 mm) on the other end of the wire. Turn
the end into a simple loop to capture the coil.

4. Place the end of one 4" (10 cm) length of 16g silver wire
onto the bench block. Hammer ¼" (6 mm) of one end.
Grip the end of the hammered end with the round-nose
pliers. Make a simple loop. String one 1" (2.5 cm) length of
coil and 1 spacer bead. Pass the wire through one loop of
the element made in Step 3, working from the outside in.
String one 13mm bead. Continue to pass the wire (from
the inside out) through the second loop of the element
made in Step 3, gently bending that element in half. String
1 spacer and one 1" (2.5 cm) coil. Hammer ¼" (6 mm) of the
end of the wire. Use the round-nose pliers to turn a simple
loop.

5. Repeat Step 4 four more times for a total of 5 sections
with focal beads.

6. Clasp: Place the end of the 2" (5 cm) length of 16g silver
wire onto the bench block. Hammer ¼" (6 mm) of one end.
Make a large simple loop on that end. Place the wire in the
round-nose pliers at the fattest part of the jaws, with the
wire positioned so that the top of the large simple loop is
just below the jaws. Bend the wire over one barrel of the
pliers to make a hook, which will be your clasp.

7. Open the simple loop formed in Step 6 and link it through
the two loops on the end of the bracelet to bring the ends
of the last element made in Step 5 together. Slip one 1"
(2.5 cm) coil section onto the hook, pushing it down as far
it will go. Hammer ¼" (6 mm) of the other end of the hook.
Make the end into a simple loop to form a decorative end
that faces away from the clasp.

This simple necklace is a study in contrasts—between copper and silver and between the undulating bent wire and the symmetry of the beads. It may be helpful to sketch the spiral before beginning and use it as a guide when you bend the wire.

asian wisdom

ronna sarvas weltman

TECHNIQUES USED
oxidizing, page 23
simple loops, page 15
wrapped loops, page 16

MATERIALS
1' (30.5 cm) of oxidized copper 16-gauge wire
1 silver 10 x 25mm bead
1 turquoise 13 x 9mm bead
1 green 31mm serpentine charm
18" (45.5 cm) copper chain necklace with clasp

TOOLS
Round-nose pliers

FINISHED SIZE
3¾" (9.5 cm) pendant

Oxidize the copper wire before making the pendant. Copper and silver cannot be oxidized together, and turquoise can be damaged by liver of sulfur.

1. Make a simple loop on one end of the wire. Attach the charm to the simple loop. Bend about 4" (10 cm) of wire above the loop back and forth to form an abstract squiggle. End the squiggle in the middle—directly over the simple loop for the charm—and bend the wire straight up.

2. String the turquoise bead and oblong silver bead on the top of the wire squiggle. Make a wrapped loop and continue to wrap the end around the top of the bead.

3. Slip the pendant onto the chain.

In this free-form cuff, there are no set rules other than to stretch your creativity and discover all the wonderful ways that wire can be wrapped and twisted to create a truly unique piece of art.

encrusted cuff

jodi l. bombardier

TECHNIQUES USED

hammering, page 15
coiling, page 18

MATERIALS

17" (43 cm) sterling silver 12-gauge dead-soft wire
20–25' (6–7.5m) sterling silver 26-gauge dead-soft wire
4 (40.5 cm) rose quartz 8mm beads
16" (40.5 cm) white 6mm top-drilled freshwater pearls
16" (40.5 cm) pink 6mm side-drilled freshwater pearls
64" (162.5 cm) white 2mm top-drilled freshwater pearls
25–30 assorted crystal and white 4mm bicone crystals
25–30 Bali silver daisy spacers

TOOLS

Flush cutters
Chain-nose pliers
Ball-peen hammer
Steel bench block
Rawhide mallet (optional)
Bracelet mandrel (optional)

FINISHED SIZE

6½" (16.5 cm)

1. Frame: Make a 90° bend 1" (2.5 cm) from one end of the 12g wire. Make a 90° bend 6¼" (16 cm) from that bend. Make another 90° bend 1" (2.5 cm) from the last bend and a 90° bend 6¼" (16 cm) from that bend to complete the rectangle, leaving a 2½" (6.5 cm) tail overlapping the other end.

2. With the ball-peen hammer, flatten the two overlapping segments. Cut off excess wire at the tail so that these two segments are both 1" (1.5 cm). Hammer the 6¼" (16 cm) sides with a rawhide mallet or texture the sides with the hammer in order to stiffen, or work-harden, these sides.

3. Cut 18" (45.5 cm) of 26g wire. Holding the overlapping 12g segments together, coil them together with the 26g wire until the entire length is wrapped. Clip off excess 26g wire and use chain-nose pliers to gently squeeze the wire end flush with frame.

4. Cut 3' (91.5 cm) of 26g wire. Coil the opposite end side so that the two ends match, but don't cut off any excess wire.

5. Embellishment: With the excess 26g wire in the corner of the frame, string a random selection of mixed beads and spacers, leaving ⅒–⅛" (2–3 mm) of bare wire. Cross diagonally to the other side of the frame and wrap once or twice around the opposite side of the frame.

6. Continue stringing beads and wrapping around the opposite side of the frame, following a zigzag pattern to the other end of the cuff and ending again at a corner.

7. String 2 or 3 of the smaller beads onto the wire and wrap around the end. Repeat several times until the end is covered with beads and wire. When you run out of 26g wire, cut another 2–3' (61–91.5 cm) of 26g wire, wrap one end onto the frame, and continue adding and wrapping beads to the frame.

8. Continue working in a zigzag back across the cuff, wrapping around the frame and the bare sections of zigzag wire. Wrap beads around the longer sides of the frame as for the shorter sides in Step 7. Continue wrapping around the frame and the existing zigzags until all gaps are filled.

9. Using your wrist or a bracelet mandrel, gently bend down the sides to shape.

Most wire cages are made to wrap a bead, but they can be quite fun on their own. Toss in a pop of fun color with this easy wire necklace. With this no-clasp design, the cording is easily interchangeable to match your mood.

so cagey!

kerry bogert

kerry bogert

TECHNIQUES USED

simple loops, page 15
coiling, page 18

MATERIALS

7½' (2.3 m) of sterling silver 16-gauge dead-soft wire
24–28" (61–71 cm) of silk cording
2 silver large-hole spacer beads

TOOLS

Round-nose pliers
Flat-nose pliers
Flush cutters
Needle file
Rotary tumbler
Stainless steel shot

FINISHED SIZE

27¾" (70.5 cm)

1. Cut 18 pieces of 16g wire to 5" (12.5 cm) lengths. Flush cut each end and file smooth.

2. Form a simple loop in opposite directions on each end of 1 wire piece; the loop should be large enough to easily fit over the silk cording.

3. Using flat-nose pliers, make 1 coil on one end but keep the coil open rather then tightly closed. Coil the other end once in the opposite direction, as if making a large loopy letter S. Continue working each end in turn, bending them in toward the center, until all the wire is coiled.

4. Fold the S in half at the center so that the two swirls sit against each other. Pull out the small center loops from each side to form an open cage bead.

5. Repeat Steps 2–4 with the remaining 17 pieces of wire.

6. Work-harden the wire cages in a rotary tumbler with stainless steel shot for about 1 hour.

7. Once dry, string the wire cages onto the silk cording. Tie an overhand knot about 2" (5 cm) from each end. String 1 bead on each end and finish with another overhand knot. The wire cages should be able to slide freely along the cording.

Placing a piece of tape around a piece of wire prevents that taped section from twisting with the rest of the wire. That's how you get the smooth "pulley" in these earrings. The briolette stones form the weights.

TECHNIQUES USED

simple loops, page 15
briolette loops, page 17
opening and closing jump rings, page 19

pretty pulleys
sandra lupo

MATERIALS

8–10" (20.5–25.5cm) of gold-filled 22-gauge dead-soft
square wire, cut in two equal lengths
10–12" (25.5–30.5 cm) of gold-filled 26-gauge
dead-soft round wire
6 blue 4x9mm briolettes
2 gold-filled 22-gauge 4mm ID jump rings
2 gold-filled ear wires

TOOLS

Flush cutters
Pin vise
Round-nose pliers
Chain-nose pliers
Stepped forming
pliers
Masking tape,
1" (2.5 cm) wide

FINISHED SIZE

2¾" (7 cm)

1. Secure 1 piece of 22g square wire in the pin vise. Measure 1½" (3.8 cm) down on each piece of 22g wire from the chuck of the vise and place a piece of tape there, covering 1" (2.5 cm) of wire. Fold the tape evenly over the wire; this will prevent that area, which will later become the pulley, from being twisted. Twist one end until there is 1¼" (3.2 cm) of twisted wire after the taped section. Note your twist count when you have made as tight a twist as you'd like. Repeat for the second part of the wire. You can choose to maintain the same tightness of twist on this side of the tape as the first side or vary the twist. Repeat with the second earring.

2. Turn a simple loop at both ends of each wire.

3. Remove the tape from the wire. Place the beginning of the untwisted portion of one 22g square wire within the jaws of the forming pliers. Wrap the wire around the round jaw until the untwisted wire is completely wrapped, or two to three full circles around the forming pliers. Repeat for second earring.

4. Wrap the briolettes with the 26g wire. Add 1 briolette to the simple loop at one end of each twisted wire and add 2 briolettes to the simple loop at the other end to create the "weighted" look. Repeat for second earring.

5. Attach the center pulley loop of each wire to an ear wire with a jump ring.

VARIATION: You may also dangle one briolette from a jump ring attached to the pulley circle.

The length and the sophisticated wire wrapping of these earrings make them an elegant addition to your jewelry box. Embellish them with any beads you like for a personal touch.

exclamation points
denise peck

MATERIALS
3" (7.5 cm) of sterling silver 18-gauge dead-soft round wire
10" (25.5 cm) of sterling silver 20-gauge dead-soft round or twisted wire
2 sterling silver head pins
2 decorative beads
2 sterling silver ear wires

TOOLS
Flush cutters
Chain-nose pliers
Awl
Ball-peen hammer
Steel bench block

FINISHED SIZE
2½" (6.5 cm) silver pair,
2⅜" (6 cm) blue pair

TECHNIQUES USED
hammering, page 15
piercing, page 23
coiling, page 18
wrapped loops, page 16
opening and closing jump rings, page 19

1. Cut the 18g wire into two 1½" (3.8 cm) lengths. Hammer flat all ends.

2. With the awl, make a hole on each flattened end to accommodate 20g wire.

3. Coil the 20g wire tightly and closely around one 18g wire so that none of the thicker wire shows through.

4. Flush cut the end of the 20g wire when the full length of the 18g wire is covered between the flat ends. If necessary, flush cut the other end to make it lie flat. Gently pinch each end with chain-nose pliers to secure. Repeat Steps 3 and 4 for the second earring.

5. Thread 1 bead on 1 head pin, pass through the hole of 1 flat end, and make a wrapped loop. Repeat for the second earring.

6. Attach 1 ear wire to the other end of each earring.

Colorful charms slide along the links of this bracelet, creating movement and a delightful jingle. The bracelet shown here is made with five S-shaped links, though the length can be adjusted by adding or removing S elements.

simply charming
tamara l. honaman

MATERIALS

23" (58.5 cm) of sterling silver 14-gauge half-hard wire

22 assorted beads

5 assorted pendants

44 Bali silver 5mm daisy spacers

44 sterling silver 3mm round beads

22 sterling silver 20-gauge head pins

9 sterling silver 18-gauge 6mm ID jump rings

TOOLS

Round-nose pliers

Chain-nose pliers

Flat-nose pliers

Heavy-duty wire cutters

Ball-peen hammer

Steel bench block

FINISHED SIZE

8" (20.5 cm)

1. S elements: Flush cut four to six 3" (7.5 cm) lengths of 14g wire. Hammer ¼" (6 mm) of each end of the wires.

2. Using round-nose pliers, coil both ends of each wire into simple loops facing in opposite directions.

3. Using round-nose pliers, bend each piece into a squat S shape, leaving the ends about 1" (2.5 cm) long.

4. Line up the S shapes in the desired order for the bracelet. Open 1 jump ring, pass through the simple loops at the end of two S shapes, and close the jump ring. Repeat to connect all S shapes with jump rings.

5. Clasp: Make a simple hook clasp and a figure-eight link with 5" (12.5 cm) of 14g wire. Attach the hook and eye with jump rings to each end of the bracelet.

6. Pendants: Use jump rings to attach one pendant to the loop on each S in the bracelet.

7. Dangles: On a head pin string 1 daisy spacer, 1 bead, 1 daisy spacer, and one 3mm round bead. Attach the dangle to a curve in one S with a wrapped loop. Repeat to add dangles all over the bracelet as desired. Dangles can also be attached to jump rings.

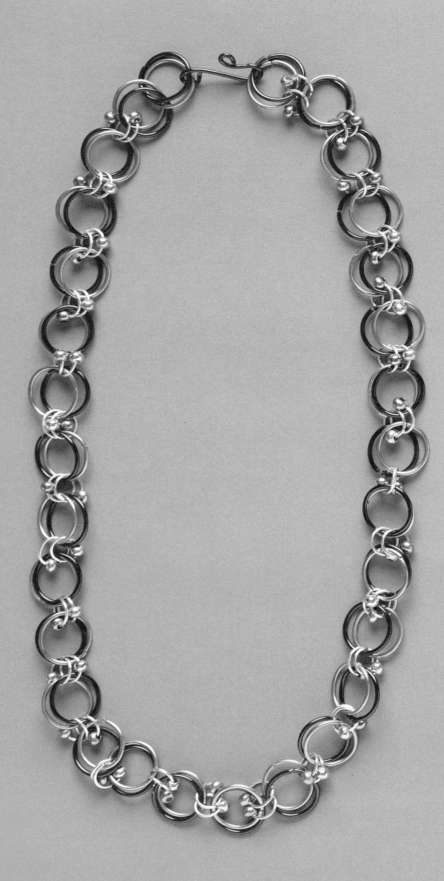

A simple chain of jump rings blossoms when you add beads
and larger rings all the way around. Added interest comes from
using three different colors of wire: silver, brass, and copper.

king of rings
linda gettings

TECHNIQUES USED
making jump rings, page 19
opening and closing jump rings, page 19
simple hooks, page 22

MATERIALS
Sterling silver 20-gauge wire
Brass 16-gauge wire
Dark copper 16-gauge wire
20 copper 4mm beads
20 silver 4mm beads
20 brass 4mm beads

TOOLS
14mm and 8mm round dowels
Flush cutters
Round-nose pliers
2 chain-nose pliers

FINISHED SIZE
23" (58.5 cm)

1. Wind the brass and copper wire into coils on the 14mm
dowel to make jump rings. Cut into 30 brass and 30
copper jump rings.

2. Wind the silver wire into coils on the 8mm dowel to
make 56 silver jump rings.

3. Close all the copper and brass jump rings.

4. String 1 metal bead onto every silver jump ring, leaving
them open.

5. String 1 copper and 1 brass jump ring onto 2 silver jump
rings and close. Connect pairs of copper and brass rings
with a pair of silver rings for the desired length of the
necklace.

6. Make a simple hook and attach to one end of the chain
for closure.

Free-form art has an appealing sense of movement that feels spontaneous. To achieve a loose work of art that looks natural but intentional, keep the lines flowing when weaving this miniature basket.

catch-all

ronna sarvas weltman

TECHNIQUES USED

coiling, page 18

spiraling, page 18

opening and closing jump rings, page 19

spiral hooks, page 22

MATERIALS

Gold-filled 16-gauge dead-soft wire
Gold-filled 18-gauge dead-soft wire
Gold-filled 20-gauge half-hard wire
2' (61 cm) of gold-filled chain
3 gold-filled 6mm jump rings

TOOLS

Flush cutters
Round-nose pliers
Chain-nose pliers
Nylon-jaw straightening pliers

FINISHED SIZE

27" (68.5 cm) necklace, 2⅜" (6 cm) pendant

1. Rim: Bend the 16g wire into a free-form double oval for the rim of the basket. This one is about 2" (5 cm) in diameter. Leaving a 2" (5 cm) tail at each end, flush cut the ends.

2. Holding the loops of the rim together, coil one of the wire tails around both loops to hold them together.

3. Vertical spokes: Wrap the end of the 18g wire around the rim a few times on the opposite side from the decorative coils. Wrap snugly so the wire will hold the rim in place.

4. Extend the wire about 2" (5 cm) down from the rim and bend it back up to the other side of the rim, forming a U shape. Flush cut the wire, leaving a 2" (5 cm) tail. Wrap the tail around the rim a few times on the opposite side.

When working with lengths of thinner gauge wire, it's easy to accidentally kink the wire. Straighten out kinks by firmly grasping the wire beyond the kink with the straightening pliers and then pulling the wire through.

5. Repeat Step 3 to make another spoke perpendicular to the first one. Where the second wire crosses the first at the bottom, wrap the second wire around the first wire a few times before bending it back up to the other side.

6. Horizontal wires: Cut a piece of 18g wire long enough to wrap horizontally around the vertical spokes a few times. Wrap one end a few times around the crossed spokes at the bottom of the basket to hold them together and to anchor the wire, then wrap the wire around one of the vertical spokes once to attach it. Build the horizontal lines by wrapping the wire around the vertical spokes, making one loop around each spoke to keep the wire firmly in place. Finish the 18g wire by wrapping the end of the tail around the rim.

7. Mesh: Cut a piece of 20g wire about 2' (61 cm) long and affix it to the rim of the necklace by wrapping a few coils around the rim. Work the wire all around the necklace, wrapping once around each spoke to keep the wire firmly in place. Any time it crosses another piece of wire, wrap the 20g wire around it. Continue wrapping, cutting more pieces of wire as needed, until the mesh is complete.

8. Coil 20g wire around the tails of the rim—coil about 2" (5 cm) around the longer tail and about 1" (2.5 cm) around the shorter tail, and loosely form the tails into decorative spirals.

9. Using round-nose pliers, grasp the wire mesh pieces and give a little turn or pinches in each piece of wire. This will also help stiffen, or work-harden, the wire.

10. Make a spiral hook with 4" (10 cm) of 18g wire.

11. Attach half the chain to one side of the basket and the other half of the chain to the other side with jump rings. Add the spiral hook to one end.

rolling rings

kerry bogert

Create a chunky necklace of interlocking rings that rolls around a neckline. The size is easily adjusted by snagging any ring with the hook clasp. Oxidizing the wire highlights the handwrought construction.

TECHNIQUES USED

hammering, page 15
wrapped loops, page 16
oxidizing, page 23

MATERIALS

9' (2.7 m) of sterling silver 18-gauge dead-soft wire
16 mottled black 3.3cm large-hole lampworked glass rings

TOOLS

Flush cutters
Round-nose pliers
Chain-nose pliers
Needle file
Ball-peen hammer
Steel bench block
¾" (2cm) mandrel
Liver of sulfur
Polishing cloth

FINISHED SIZE

21" (53.5 cm)

1. Cut seventeen 6" (15 cm) pieces of wire. Shape each piece into a ring by wrapping it once around the mandrel at the center of the wire, leaving the crossed ends long.

2. Using a ball-peen hammer and bench block, stiffen the rings by hammering the round area of each ring up to the section where the ends cross.

3. Slightly separate the ends of 1 wire ring and string 1 glass ring. Make a wrapped loop on one end near where the wires cross.

4. Pass the other end through the center of the wrapped loop and wrap it to close. Trim and file any sharp ends of cut wire.

5. Repeat Steps 3 and 4 for desired length, slipping 1 previously connected glass ring and 1 new glass ring onto each wire ring. End with 1 glass ring and reserve 1 wire ring for the clasp.

6. Clasp: Attach the reserved wire link to the last glass ring with the last wire link. Make a wrapped loop with one end, then pass the other end through the loop. Instead of making a second wrapped loop, use round-nose pliers to form a hook with the wire. Trim the excess wire and form a small closed loop on the end of the trimmed wire.

7. Hammer the arch of the hook.

8. Dip the finished necklace in liver of sulfur solution to oxidize the sterling silver wire. The liver of sulfur solution should be warm, not hot; hot water can cause thermal shock and crack the lampworked beads. Polish the piece to highlight the wirework, leaving grooved areas blackened.

Coiling adds a nice texture to any piece of wire jewelry. Use this simple technique to create a frame around colorful stone nuggets, then coil some or coil them all to create a lively bib-style necklace.

framed and coiled

jodi l. bombardier

TECHNIQUES USED:

straightening wire, page 14

wrapped loops, page 16

coiling, page 18

opening and closing jump rings, page 19

MATERIALS

8½" (2.6 m) of 22-gauge sterling silver dead-soft wire

20' (6.1 m) of sterling silver 28-gauge dead-soft wire

13 amazonite 2.5–3cm nuggets

28" (71 cm) of sterling silver chain with 18mm and 6mm round links

14 sterling silver 5mm jump rings

1 toggle clasp

TOOLS

Nylon-jaw straightening pliers

Flush cutters

Chain-nose pliers

Round-nose pliers

FINISHED SIZE

21" (53.5 cm)

VARIATION: You could make a necklace of individual framed nuggets joined with jump rings.

1. Uncoiled frames: Cut and straighten 8" (20.5 cm) of 22g wire. Make a wrapped loop and string 1 nugget. Make another wrapped loop on the other side of the bead. Gently pull the excess wire around the nugget, wrap the wire once around the base of the first wrapped loop, and gently pull the wire around to the second wrapped loop. Wrap the wire once around the base of the second loop and clip off any remaining wire. With chain-nose pliers, gently squeeze the end of the wire to flatten it as closely as possible to the wrapped loop. Repeat entire step for a total of 4 uncoiled frames.

2. Coiled frames: Cut 8" (20.5 cm) of 22g wire (frame wire). Make a wrapped loop and string on a nugget. Make another wrapped loop on the other side of the bead. Cut 18" (45.5 cm) of 28g wire (coil wire). Wrap the tail of the coil wire once around the base of the wrapped loop. Coil around the frame wire to the other wrapped loop. Wrap the end of the coil wire around the base of the wrapped loop and cut. Repeat for the second half of the frame. Make 1 more single coiled nugget.

3. Make 4 groups of 2 nuggets looped together, mixing coiled and uncoiled nuggets: Follow the directions above to make the first coiled nugget. Before you close and wrap the first loop, slip the loop onto a loop of a completed uncoiled nugget. Make the centerpiece of 3 coiled framed nuggets in the same manner. The frame will become a bit misshapen while coiling. When the nugget frame is completely coiled, reshape the coiled frame, using your fingers or chain-nose pliers to gently squeeze the frame back into alignment and shape.

4. Cut and measure chain to desired lengths. Attach the lengths of chain to the nuggets and the toggle clasp with jump rings.

Curves galore and a handmade clasp bring these lampworked beads together for a striking effect. Accented with sterling silver spacer beads, the lampworked beads really make a statement. This is a bracelet that can easily be transformed into a necklace—just make more links!

LEVEL 2

coiled again!
tamara l. honaman

TECHNIQUES USED
hammering, page 15
simple hooks, page 20
spiraling, page 18
opening and closing jump rings, page 19
figure-eight links, page 20

MATERIALS
21" (53.5 cm) of sterling silver 16-gauge half-hard wire
4" (10 cm) of sterling silver 14-gauge half-hard wire
7 multicolored 13 x 8mm lampworked beads
14 sterling silver 7mm disc spacers
2 sterling silver 16-gauge 5mm ID jump rings
6 sterling silver 16-gauge 6mm ID jump rings

TOOLS
Heavy-duty flush cutters
Round-nose pliers
Chain-nose pliers
Flat-nose pliers
Ball-peen hammer
Steel bench block

FINISHED SIZE
8⅜" (21.5 cm)

1. Cut seven 3" (7.5 cm) lengths of 16g wire so that each end is flush-cut. Place 1 wire on the steel bench block and hammer ¼" (6 mm) of one end; repeat with the remaining 6 wires.

2. Using round-nose and flat-nose pliers, spiral the hammered end for about two full revolutions. String 1 spacer, 1 lampworked bead, and 1 spacer. Hammer ¼" (6 mm) at the other end and spiral until it rests against the spacer and the beads are secured. Repeat with remaining cut wires, spacers, and lampworked beads.

3. Cut the 14g wire in half. Make a simple hook clasp with one half and a figure-eight link with the other.

4. Open one 6mm jump ring. Link the coils of 2 lampworked elements and close the jump ring. Repeat to join all the lampworked elements.

5. Use one 5mm jump ring to attach the hook clasp to one end and the other 5mm jump ring to attach the figure-eight link.

twigs

ronna sarvas weltman

This necklace combines primitive elegance, by using like elements of strong vertical and textured metal, with asymmetrical intrigue, by making each loop and wrap slightly different. The very simple cord adds modern flair and keeps the spotlight on the wirework.

MATERIALS

2' (61 cm) of sterling silver 20-gauge dead-soft wire
1 package SoftGlas tubing
1 SoftGlas connector

TOOLS

Flush cutters
Round-nose pliers
Chain-nose pliers
Ball-peen hammer
Steel bench block
Liver of sulfur
Polishing cloth

FINISHED SIZE

14½" (37 cm) cord, 3" (7.5 cm) pendants

1. Cut 5 or 6 varying lengths of wire between 2–3" (5–7.5 cm). Bend and curve each wire slightly to create differences in the twigs.

2. Hammer each piece of wire to texture and flatten, pounding more at the ends so they flare out. (Flattening and texturing the wire will work-harden and stiffen it.)

3. Using round-nose pliers, make a sloppy wrapped loop at the top of each wire. Be sure the loops are large enough to hang freely from the cord so the twigs dangle gracefully. Vary the size of the loops and the number of times each tail is wrapped.

4. Oxidize all the wire with liver of sulfur and polish lightly.

5. Cut SoftGlas tubing to desired length and attach SoftGlas connector by slipping it into one end of the hollow tubing.

6. Place the twigs on a flat surface and arrange them as desired, then string them on the cord. Using your fingers, bend the 2 twigs that flank the center twig out slightly. Bend the outer twigs a little more to create a slightly fanned shape.

twisted bracelet

howard siegel

TECHNIQUES USED
making jump rings, page 19
opening and closing jump rings, page 19

This chain must be twisted each time it's put on by holding the jump ring at the end and twisting the clasp end clockwise. Its helical shape rolls up and down your wrist as you move, accentuating the twist pattern.

MATERIALS

56" (142 cm) of sterling silver 18-gauge dead-soft wire
1 sterling silver 16-gauge $^{13}/_{64}$" (5mm) ID jump ring
1 sterling silver 16-gauge $^{17}/_{64}$" (7mm) ID jump ring
1 sterling silver 7 x 12mm lobster clasp

TOOLS

$^{13}/_{64}$" (5mm) diameter mandrel
Flush cutters
2 chain-nose pliers
Twist tie (the type used to close grocery bags)
Rotary tumbler
Stainless steel shot

FINISHED SIZE

7$^{7}/_{8}$" (20 cm)

1. Wind all the 18g silver wire into coils on the mandrel, making about fifty turns at a time so they're not too difficult to cut. Cut into jump rings.

2. Using 2 chain-nose pliers, close one of the jump rings. Insert the twist tie into the closed jump ring and twist to hold it in place. This is the starter ring.

3. Open all the other jump rings about 60°.

4. Insert 1 open jump ring through the starter ring and close.

5. Hold the starter ring in one hand and grasp the second ring with the thumb and forefinger of the other hand. Twist the chain away from you.

6. Hold the rings in the twisted position and insert a third ring through the first two rings from the back of the chain. (This is sometimes called a "one through two chain.") The rings are added from the back of the chain so that you can clearly see that the ring being added to the chain is passing through the last two rings of the chain. Close the third ring.

7. Twist the chain away from you as before and insert the fourth ring through the last two rings on the chain from the back of the chain. Close the ring.

8. Continue adding the rings from the back of the chain through the last two rings and twisting the chain after each ring is added until the chain measures 6½" (16.5 cm).

9. Open the two 16g jump rings. Twist the chain as before and insert the $^{13}/_{64}$" (5mm) 16g jump ring through the last two rings on the chain. Insert the jump ring through the end of the lobster clasp, then close the jump ring.

10. Remove the twist tie. Twist the chain away from you and insert the $^{17}/_{64}$" (7mm) 16g jump ring through the last two rings on this end of the chain, then close the jump ring.

11. Tumble the chain for about 1 hour with stainless steel shot to polish and remove any rough burrs. Remove the chain from the tumbler, rinse in clean running water, and dry with a terry towel.

elemental

sandra lupo

A collection of natural shapes in semiprecious stone, bone, shell, and tumbled rocks hangs from an embellished chain. This is a nice way to wear a collection of favorite finds, set off by beautiful handmade links.

TECHNIQUES USED
hammering, page 15
coiling, page 18
making jump rings, page 19
simple hooks, page 20

MATERIALS

3½' (1.1 m) of sterling silver 16-gauge
   dead-soft wire (for links)
3½' (1.1 m) of sterling silver 14-gauge
   dead-soft wire (for links and clasp)
Sterling silver 22-gauge dead-soft wire
Copper 22-gauge round wire
5–10 semiprecious stones, bones, shells, and
   tumbled rocks in natural shapes (drilled)

TOOLS

Flush cutters
Flat-nose pliers
Stainless steel oval bezel mandrel
Carpenter's wood pencil (available at hardware stores)
Sharpie marker
Ball-peen hammer
Steel bench block
Needle file
Rotary tumbler
Stainless steel shot
Polishing cloth

FINISHED SIZE

16" (40.5 cm)

1. Chain: Cut 1½' (3.8 cm) of 16g wire. Tape 1 wire end to the smaller end of a stainless steel oval bezel mandrel. Firmly form the wire around the mandrel with your fingers, working toward the larger end, to make a graduated coil with the whole length of wire. Before removing the coil from the mandrel, use the marker to make a vertical line down one long side of this graduated coil of wire. Remove the tape and coil.

2. Use flush cutters to cut each coil at the marks made in Step 1, keeping the rings in order of their size. File the ends flat so they close properly. Hammer some of the links for texture to give the chain some interest. Attach the rings to each other to form a graduated chain about 6" (15 cm) long. Reserve 2 small rings for a later step.

3. Repeat Steps 1 and 2 for the other side of the chain necklace. Reserve 2 small rings again for a later step. Set both chains aside.

4. Links: Use the carpenter's pencil as a mandrel to form the 14g wire into a short oval coil of wire, 2–3 coils at a time. Make a total of 5 oval links.

5. Hammer the oval links, leaving one or two sides in their original round shape. Use the ball side of the hammer to pock-mark the links for surface texture. Reshape and close each link after hammering.

6. Wrap 22g wire tightly around the cut ends of each link, using silver and copper as desired. Set the 5 rings aside.

7. Repeat Steps 4 and 5 to create 5 more large oval links; these will attach the pendants to the chain necklace. Hammer these links into a script C shape, using the flat side of the hammer to widen the wire as the link curves. Set these 5 aside.

8. Repeat Steps 4 and 5 to create 5 more large oval links; these will be jump rings to attach pendants.

9. Tumble the chain and links with stainless steel shot for a high shine.

10. Assembly: Attach each large jump ring to 1 pendant or double up small stones to form a single pendant. Slip each pendant onto a C ring. Attach each C ring to a wrapped link.

11. Attach the wrapped links to each other with the 4 small links from Step 3 and attach a piece of graduated chain to each side of the necklace.

12. Use 3" (7.5 cm) of 14g wire to make a simple hook. Hammer flat at the curve and file the ends smooth. Polish and attach to one end of the chain.

french rope

howard siegel

The slinky spiral of this popular style of chain looks much more complicated than a series of jump rings. It's sometimes called a "one through three chain" because of the manner in which it is woven.

MATERIALS

22' (6.7 m) of sterling silver 14-gauge half-round dead-soft wire

2 sterling silver 14-gauge ¼" (6mm) ID jump rings

1 sterling silver 12 x 8mm lobster clasp

TOOLS

³⁄₁₆" (5mm) diameter mandrel

Flush cutters

2 chain-nose pliers

Twist tie (the type used to close grocery bags)

Rotary tumbler

Stainless steel shot

FINISHED SIZE

29¼" (74.5 cm)

TECHNIQUES USED

making jump rings, page 19

opening and closing jump rings, page 19

1. Wind the silver wire into coils on the mandrel, making about fifty turns at a time so they're not too difficult to cut. Repeat to make 365 jump rings.

2. Close one of the jump rings using 2 chain-nose pliers. Insert the twist tie into the closed jump ring and twist to hold it in place. This is the starter ring.

3. Open all the other jump rings about 60° and sort them into groups of 13. This will enable you to track the length of the chain as you weave it.

4. Insert 1 open jump ring through the starter ring and close.

5. Hold the two joined jump rings between the thumb and forefinger of one hand while you twist the chain away from you with the thumb and forefinger of the other hand. Holding the chain in this position, insert the third jump ring from the back through the first two rings. Close the third jump ring.

6. Keeping the chain twisted away from you, insert a fourth jump ring from the back of the chain through all three of the previous rings. The rings are added from the back of the chain so that you can clearly see that the ring being added to the chain is passing through the last three rings of the chain. Close the fourth jump ring.

7. Keeping the chain twisted away from you, continue inserting the next jump ring from the back of the chain through the last three rings on the chain. Continue adding one ring at a time until chain is the desired length or until all of the jump rings have been added.

8. Open the two 14g jump rings. Twist the chain as in Step 5, insert one 14g jump ring through the last three rings on the chain, and attach the clasp. Close the ring.

9. Remove the twist tie from the other end of the chain. Twist the chain as in Step 5, insert the remaining 14g jump ring through the last three rings on the chain, and close the jump ring.

10. Tumble the chain for about an hour with stainless steel shot to polish and remove any rough burrs. Remove the chain from the tumbler, rinse in clean running water, and dry with a terry towel.

Sequins have always been a sparkling star in the fashion industry. Stacked on wire, they take on a subtle glow, but they surprise with an occasional glitter when the faces are revealed at the bends in the wire.

all that glitters
denise peck

TECHNIQUES USED

making ear wires, page 22
coiling, page 18
simple loops, page 15

MATERIALS
7" (18 cm) stack of gold sequins
9" (23 cm) of copper 20-gauge wire
6" (15 cm) of copper 24-gauge wire

TOOLS
Flush cutters
Round-nose pliers
Chain-nose pliers
Sharpie marker
Bezel mandrel
Ball-peen hammer
Steel bench block

FINISHED SIZE
2½" (6.5 cm)

1. Cut the 20g copper wire in half. Bend one end of each piece over the Sharpie or mandrel about 1" (2.5 cm) from the end to form the ear wire. Make a small outward bend at each tip with round-nose pliers.

2. With 24g copper wire, wrap a neat, tight coil around the front of each ear wire; this will act as a stopper for the sequins and add a decorative element on the wire. Flush cut each end of the coils and pinch to secure with chain-nose pliers.

3. String 3½" (9 cm) of sequins from the other end of each piece of wire, being sure all the sequins are facing the same direction as you load them.

4. Holding the sequins firmly against the coil with your fingers, gently wrap the lengths of sequined wire around the bezel mandrel or pen. Keep the sequins snugly stacked.

5. With the 24g copper wire, wrap the ends of the earrings for 12 coils, pushing it up against the stack of sequins.

6. Flush cut any remaining wire that extends past the wraps and make a small simple loop with the coiled ends.

Rethink the ordinary! If an earring is usually long in the front and short in the back, why not switch it up? Beautiful top-drilled diamond-shaped beads dangle from the short coil in the front of these earrings while the ear wires extend down behind the ear.

overwrought
denise peck

TECHNIQUES USED
hammering, page 15
simple loops, page 15
wrapped loops, page 16
briolette loops, page 17

MATERIALS
7" (18 cm) of sterling silver 19-gauge dead-soft wire
6" (16 cm) of sterling silver 26-gauge dead-soft wire
2 labradorite 7mm faceted diamond-shaped top-drilled beads

TOOLS
Flush cutters
Round-nose pliers
Ball-peen hammer
Steel bench block

FINISHED SIZE
2" (5 cm)

1. Cut the 19g silver wire in half.

2. Use round-nose pliers to curl one end, beginning with a tight simple loop that will hold the bead dangle securely. Extend the curl gently and leave the length of the wire facing down. Hammer the curl flat with the ball-peen hammer. Repeat with second piece of wire.

3. Make briolette loops with the 26g wire on each bead. Open the tight loops on the ear wires slightly to slip 1 bead dangle on each.

Create as you go with this wire- and bead-wrapped bracelet. Erinite Swarovski crystals with peacock pearls evoke a grapevine, but you could use green crystals with pink beads and make a rosebush!

grapevine
jodi l. bombardier

TECHNIQUES USED
spiraling, page 18
coiling, page 18

MATERIALS

11" (3.4 m) of 14-gauge dead-soft wire

2–3' (61–91.5 cm) of 20-gauge dead-soft wire

8–10' (2.4–3 m) of 26-gauge dead-soft wire

15–20 assorted color 4mm crystals

16" (40.5 cm) of 2mm pearls

15–20 Bali silver daisy spacers

TOOLS

Flush cutters

Round-nose pliers

Chain-nose pliers

Bracelet mandrel
  (optional)

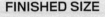

FINISHED SIZE

7" (18 cm)

1. Flush cut both ends of the 14g wire. Make a small spiral at the end of the wire. On the other end, make a spiral in the opposite direction. Measure the bracelet as you make the spirals to check the length; the spirals can be as large as the wire length allows. When the spirals and bracelet are the desired length, make 90° bends in the wire at the top of each spiral.

2. Starting at the top of a spiral where the wire is bent, coil the 20g wire several times around the 14g frame. Move about 1 cm along the frame and wrap a few more times onto the frame but do not pull the 20g wire tight against the frame. Leave the 20g wire a bit loose between the wraps so it creates a small arch alongside the frame, providing more areas to bind beads.

3. Continue wrapping 20g wire onto the frame and creating arches as in Step 2, but occasionally pull the 20g wire snug against the frame and wrap it several times to create a decorative coil. When the wraps reach the second spiral, turn the frame and work back toward the other side.

4. Cut 2–3' of 26g wire and wrap it several times onto one end of the frame. String 2–3 beads onto the wire and wrap it onto the frame or the 20g wire.

It is important to pull the wire snug as you wrap beads onto the frame. Use chain-nose pliers if necessary for a good grasp on the wire.

5. Continue stringing beads and wrapping the wire onto the frame until the end of the 26g wire. Wrap the end of the 26g wire around the frame a few times and trim as close as possible to the frame. Use chain-nose pliers to gently squeeze the end of the wire against the frame. Cut another piece of 26g wire, secure the end, and string and wrap as before. Continue until the bracelet is fully embellished or no beads remain.

6. Shape the bracelet using your wrist or a bracelet mandrel.

Wire-wrapped beaded loops and simple figure-eight links make up the
chain on this unusual necklace. Frame a beautiful pendant with dramatic
wire drops, and you have a necklace that's sure to be noticed.

sticks & stones
linda gettings

MATERIALS
5' (1.5 m) of 20-gauge copper wire
2' (61 cm) of 16-gauge dark copper-colored wire
50 copper-colored 6mm beads
100 copper 4mm beads
1 copper 2 x 4cm glass pendant

TOOLS
Flush cutters
Round-nose pliers
Chain-nose pliers
Nylon-jaw straightening pliers

FINISHED SIZE
20" (51 cm)

1. Cut twelve 3" (7.5 cm) pieces of 20g wire. Straighten
each piece with nylon-jaw pliers.

2. Make a wrapped loop at one end of each piece of 20g
wire. String one 4mm, one 6mm, and one 4mm bead.
Make a wrapped loop on the other end. Repeat entire step
eleven more times.

3. Cut twelve 1½" (3.8 cm) pieces of 16g wire. With the
fattest part of the round-nose pliers, make 12 figure-eight
links.

4. Attach one end of a wire-wrapped loop to each figure-
eight link. Make 2 chain lengths using 7 figure-eight links
and 6 wire-wrapped loop pieces.

5. Bail: Cut a piece of 16g wire about 2" (5 cm) long. Make
a simple loop on one end, string the focal bead, and make
a loop on the other end. Gently bend the bail over the
round-nose pliers. Attach the 2 chain pieces to each loop.

6. Dangles: Cut 20–24 pieces of random lengths from the
remaining 20g wire. Make a wrapped loop on one end of
each wire, string one 4mm, one 6mm, and another 4mm
bead. Repeat for all of the lengths of wire.

7. Make a simple loop at the other end of each dangle to
attach them randomly around the chain on both sides of
the pendant.

8. Clasp: Use the remaining 16g wire to make a simple
hook and a 9mm jump ring. Attach to the ends of the
chain.

ribbons bracelet
kerry bogert

The links in this design will build your skills in making consistently sized components. Made correctly, these links will look like a ribbon of silver flowing through the design. This is a perfect way to showcase a few special beads.

TECHNIQUES USED

simple loops, page 15
simple hooks, page 20
wrapped loops, page 16

MATERIALS

2½' (76 cm) of sterling silver 18-gauge dead-soft wire
3 mottled amber 18–20mm lampworked coins
6 silver 4mm coiled spacers
6 silver 4mm daisy spacers

TOOLS

Flush cutters
Round-nose pliers
Chain-nose pliers
Needle file
Rawhide mallet
Steel bench block
Bracelet mandrel

FINISHED SIZE

7⅞" (20 cm)

1. Cut six 2¼" (5.5 cm) pieces of wire and three 4" (10 cm) pieces. File rough ends.

2. With round-nose pliers, make simple loops at the ends of each 2¼" (5.5 cm) piece of wire so that they face each other.

3. Using a bracelet mandrel, bend a gentle arch in all the pieces. Work-harden the arched links by hammering them with the mallet and steel bench block.

4. Using a 4" (10 cm) length of wire and round-nose pliers, make a triangular wrapped loop by using the flat side of the jaws and the edge of the jaws to bend the tip into a triangle, but before closing the loop, string 3 of the coiled ends of the arched pieces. String 1 coiled spacer, 1 daisy spacer, 1 bead, 1 daisy spacer, and 1 coiled spacer and close the other end as for the first, passing through the remaining 3 arched wire pieces and making a wrapped loop.

5. With each remaining 4" (10 cm) piece, make a wrapped loop that passes through three loose ends of the arched lengths. String 1 coiled spacer, 1 daisy spacer, 1 bead, 1 daisy spacer, and 1 coiled spacer and close with a larger round wrapped loop.

6. Make a simple hook clasp and attach it to one end.

To show off the beautiful coloring of the stone, this cage pendant is simple and understated—the wire adds interest without diminishing the appeal of the stone. Vary the gauge depending on the size of the stone and the desired look.

finders keepers
ronna sarvas weltman

TECHNIQUES USED
simple loops, page 15
wrapped loops, page 16
hammering, page 15
coiling, page 18
making jump rings, page 19

MATERIALS

1 found 20 x 25mm stone
1½' (45.5 cm) of 18-gauge sterling silver dead-soft wire
1' (30.5 cm) of 20-gauge sterling silver dead-soft wire
1' (30.5 cm) of 24-gauge sterling silver dead-soft wire
3 green silk 30" (76 cm) cords

TOOLS

Flush cutters
Round-nose pliers
Ball-peen hammer
Steel bench block
8mm mandrel

FINISHED SIZE

30½" (77.5 cm) necklace
2" (5 cm) pendant

1. On one end of 10" (25.5 cm) of 18g wire, make a simple loop large enough to accommodate the silk ribbons. Wrap the wire all the way around the outside of the stone to form a frame, leaving a small space between the wire and the stone. When the wire reaches the simple loop, wrap the end twice around the base of the simple loop and flush cut the end.

2. Coil one end of the 20g wire two to three times around the frame near the bail. Bring the wire over to the other side of frame and wrap again two to three times, being sure that the wire is curved outward to accommodate the stone.

3. Holding the stone inside the frame, wrap the 20g wire across to the other side of the frame, and then secure it again with two to three wraps around the frame. Continue crossing over the stone on both sides of the frame to form a cage. To finish, wrap the 20g wire two to three times around the 18g wire frame and flush cut near the frame.

4. Continue wrapping the stone to the frame using the 24g wire. To keep the cage in place, loop the 24g wire once firmly around each wire that it crosses on the stone and two to three times on the frame.

5. When the stone is secure within the cage, wrap the end of the 24g wire around the frame and flush cut.

6. Tweak the mesh to give it more curves. Hold the wire with round-nose pliers and twist slightly to bend the wire into a curve. Continue twisting and bending the mesh wires to achieve an undulating effect. Slip the pendant into the neck cord.

Fine-gauge wire wraps tiny faceted tourmaline beads to this long ear wire and makes a simple yet elegant uninterrupted column of stones.

tourmaline columns
denise peck

TECHNIQUES USED
coiling, page 18
hammering, page 15

MATERIALS
6" (15 cm) of 20-gauge sterling silver half-hard wire, cut in
   half
14" (35.5 cm) of 28-gauge sterling silver half-hard wire
26 tourmaline 2 x 3mm faceted coins

TOOLS
Flush cutters
Flat-nose pliers
Ball-peen hammer
Steel bench block

FINISHED SIZE
1¾" (4.5 cm)

1. With flat-nose pliers, make a sharp bend near the halfway mark of 1 piece of 20g wire leaving one side a tiny bit longer than the other.

2. With your fingers, gently curve both sides.

3. Hammer the end of the longer side flat on the bench block.

4. Beginning ⅛" (3 mm) from the bend on the longer side of the earring, coil the 28g wire tightly three times around the 20g wire. String 1 bead on the 26g wire and wrap the finer wire once around the ear wire to anchor. String another bead and wrap to anchor. Repeat for the length of the wire, ending with 3 tight coils to match the top.

5. Repeat Steps 1–4 for the second earring, making the bent portion of the ear wire as similar to the first earring as possible.

These earrings use only one wire each, with the ear wire made from the same wire as the decorative spiral. The 20-gauge sterling silver manufactured twisted wire has a good amount of body and functions well for ear wires.

singular sensation

sandra lupo

MATERIALS

2 glass or stone 12 x 14mm flat-faced beads
  (bead hole should be .75mm to accommodate wire)
20" (51 cm) of sterling silver 20-gauge twisted half-hard
  wire, cut in 2 equal lengths

TOOLS

Flush cutters
Round-nose pliers
Flat-nose pliers
Chain-nose pliers
Needle file
Sharpie marker

FINISHED SIZE

1⅛" (3 mm)

Perform each step on both pieces of wire concurrently. Once you have done a step on one wire, repeat it on the other wire. This will assure you have consistently shaped wires.

1. Mark 4" (10 cm) from one end of each wire. Fold each wire over the smaller end of the round-nose pliers at those marks. The wires will be parallel with a curve at the bend; pinch the two ends of each wire together to resemble a bobby pin.

2. With the bend of the wire held firmly in the flat-nose pliers, begin to swirl both sides of the wire into a spiral, keeping them tight together as they curve. Continue until the spiral is the size of the bead surface, leaving a long and short tail. Repeat with the second wire.

3. Pass the longer wire tail through the bead and gently bend the wire so that the spiral rests on the surface of the bead. Repeat with the other wire and bead, but reverse the spiral direction.

4. Press the spirals onto the faces of the beads and bend the shorter tails to stick up off the tops of the beads.

5. Form the ear wires by bending the longer tails over the marker. Trim them to the same length and use a needle file to smooth the ends that goes through the ear. Make a slight bend at the end of each ear wire with chain-nose pliers.

6. Wrap the short wires several times around the bases of the ear wire and flush cut.

This frame bracelet is a great starter project for the jewelry artist who is new to wire wrapping. It is easy to lengthen the bracelet by adding a bend or two on the frame before wrapping on beads.

opal waves
jodi l. bombardier

TECHNIQUES USED

straightening wire, page 14
simple loops, page 15
coiling, page 18
spiraling, page 18
simple hooks, page 20

MATERIALS

17" (43 cm) of sterling silver 16-gauge half-hard wire
3' (91.5 cm) of sterling silver 26-gauge half-hard wire
15 round 8mm Peruvian opals

TOOLS

Nylon-jaw straightening pliers
Flush cutters
Size N metal crochet hook or 9mm round mandrel
Round-nose pliers
Chain-nose pliers
Bracelet mandrel (optional)

FINISHED SIZE

7" (18 cm)

1. Frame: Use nylon-jaw pliers to straighten the 16g wire and flush cut 14" (33.5 cm). Make a simple loop at one end.

2. Using round-nose pliers, pull the wire back and around from the simple loop made to create a small wave-shaped loop in your frame. This brings the wire into position to start shaping the frame for the larger waves.

3. Bend the wire over the 9mm mandrel to start making the wave-shaped bends in the frame. Keep the bends as uniform as possible.

4. Continue bending the wire back and forth in undulating waves until it measures about 6" (15 cm) long. The bracelet frame shown here has 15 bends, leaving a tail about 2½" (6.5 cm) long.

5. Bend the tail up 90° after the last wave. Coil the end of the tail around the fattest part of the jaws of the round-nose pliers, then make more coils outside the first one. Continue looping until 1" (2.5 cm) of wire remains between the loop and the 90° angle.

6. Grip the wire with the chain-nose pliers about ¼" (6 mm) from the loop and bend the wire over the jaw to form a triangular eye loop.

7. Straighten and flush cut 3' (91.5 cm) of 26g round wire. Starting at the end of the frame with the simple loop, coil the 26g wire around the frame five to six times, then string a bead on the wire.

8. Wrap the 26g wire around the next section of the frame five to six times and string the next bead onto the wire. Continue wrapping wire and stringing beads to the end of the frame. Cut the end of the 26g wire flush to the frame.

9. With 16g wire, make a simple hook. Open the simple loop on the bracelet, slip on the hook, and close the loop.

10. Using your wrist or a bracelet mandrel, gently bend down the sides to shape.

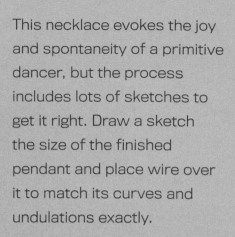

This necklace evokes the joy and spontaneity of a primitive dancer, but the process includes lots of sketches to get it right. Draw a sketch the size of the finished pendant and place wire over it to match its curves and undulations exactly.

TECHNIQUES USED
hammering, page 15
coiling, page 18

MATERIALS
3½' (1.1 m) of gold-filled 14-gauge dead-soft wire
12" (30.5 cm) of gold-filled 20-gauge dead-soft wire
4' (1.2 m) of gold-filled 22-gauge dead-soft wire

TOOLS
Flush cutters
Round-nose pliers
Chain-nose pliers
Ball-peen hammer
Steel bench block

FINISHED SIZE
14" (35.5 cm) collar,
5¼" (13.5 cm) pendant

dance all night

ronna sarvas weltman

1. Sketch a design evoking a primitive dancer. If necessary, reproduce it to the exact size of the desired pendant.

2. Lay the 14g wire on top of the sketch, bending it to match the curves in the sketch and cutting it to the exact size. Repeat for the cross pieces. Flush cut the ends of all the pieces.

3. Hammer each piece of wire to flatten and texture it. Hammer the ends slightly more so they flare out.

4. Lash the cross pieces to the longer frame with the 22g wire by placing a crosspiece on the larger frame and wrapping the 22g wire around both pieces about three times, then crossing the wire to wrap diagonally the other way, forming a wire X at each intersection. Repeat until each horizontal crosspiece of wire is attached to the torso piece. Use chain-nose pliers to tuck the ends of the wire firmly down on the back of the piece.

5. Use 22g wire to create the mesh dress fabric. Starting at the first, top intersection of the frame and a crosspiece, wrap the end of the 22g wire twice around the outside frame to attach it and use the chain-nose pliers to tuck the end to the back side of the piece firmly. Cross the wire over to the other side of the frame and loop it around once to affix it. Continue crisscrossing and re-crossing randomly to form a mesh. Each time wire crosses wire, loop it around firmly at the intersection to keep the mesh in place.

6. Using round-nose pliers, grasp the wire mesh pieces and give them each a little turn or pinch in each piece of wire. This will also help work-harden the wire.

7. To create fringe on the hemline of the dress, cut pieces of 20g wire a little more than twice the length of the desired fringe. (You'll lose a bit of length twisting and curving the pieces.) Vary the lengths to add movement. Hammer and texture the ends, hammering the tips more so they flare out, but do not hammer the middle.

8. Using round-nose pliers, bend a fringe wire in half. Hook it over the bottom frame and twist it once or twice to hold it in place, being sure that the loop is loose enough for the dangles to sway.

9. For the doubled necklace portion, cut the 14g wire into two 1¾' (53.5 cm) lengths and hammer them both to flatten and texture, pounding the ends more to flare the ends. Shape the wires together to form a collar. The pieces should be very similar but not identical. Coil 20g wire near the end of each side to bind the pieces together, then bend the ends of the necklace apart slightly so they flare out.

10. The pendant hangs from a loosely coiled bail on the outer neck wire, which is in turn attached to a bail on the inner neck wire. Pound and flatten 2" (5 cm) of 20g wire, working the ends more to flare out. To attach the pendant to the outer neck wire, hold both the pendant and the neck wire. Use round-nose pliers to coil the 2" (5 cm) piece of wire loosely around the top of the pendant and the outer neck wire about four times. Be sure that the circumference of the coil is large enough to allow the pendant to dangle freely.

11. With a 2" (5 cm) piece of 20g wire, make 3 tight coils on the inner neck wire. Thread the end of the 20g wire through the center two coils of the lower bail, then make 3 more tight coils on the inner neck wire. Use chain-nose pliers to tuck the ends in neatly.

This sturdy chain requires two different sizes of jump rings made from the same-gauge wire. Three layers of large jump rings are held together by pairs of perpendicular smaller rings, giving this chain-maille piece a new dimension.

unparalleled
howard siegel

MATERIALS

22½' (6.7 m) of sterling silver 16-gauge dead-soft wire
1 sterling silver 14mm lobster clasp

TOOLS

7mm mandrel
4.5mm mandrel
Flush cutters
2 chain-nose pliers
1 twist tie (the type used to close grocery bags)
Rotary tumbler
Stainless steel shot

FINISHED SIZE

25½" (65 cm)

1. Measure 15½' (4.7 m) of wire for the 7mm coils. Wind the silver wire into coils on the 7mm mandrel, making about fifty turns at a time so they're not too difficult to cut. Repeat to make 180 jump rings.

2. Measure 6½' (2 m) for the 4.5mm coils. Wind the silver wire into coils on the 4.5mm mandrel, making about fifty turns at a time so they're not too difficult to cut. Repeat to make 120 jump rings.

3. Open all the jump rings about 60°.

4. With chain-nose pliers, close two of the 7mm rings, insert the twist tie into the closed jump rings and twist to hold it in place. Place two 4.5mm jump rings through the two large jump rings and close both.

5. Insert a 7mm jump ring between the 7mm jump rings and around the two 4.5mm jump rings from Step 4 and close the ring. This third large jump ring will surround the two small jump rings.

6. Insert two 7mm jump rings through the two 4.5mm jump rings, one on top of the ring from Step 5 and one underneath it. Close both.

7. Place two small 4.5mm jump rings through the two 7mm jump rings added in Step 6 and close both.

8. Insert a 7mm jump ring between the two 7mm jump rings and around the two 4.5 mm jump rings added in Step 7 and close the ring.

9. Repeat Steps 6–8 until the chain is the desired length, ending with Step 6.

10. Open the last 2 jump rings on the chain, add the lobster clasp, and close them.

11. Remove the twist tie from the chain. The clasp will go through the two 7mm jump rings with which the chain was started.

12. Tumble the chain for about 1 hour with stainless steel shot and burnishing compound to polish and remove any rough burrs. Remove the chain from the tumbler, rinse in clean running water, and dry with a terry towel.

When working with wire, some things you try won't turn out exactly as you'd hoped. This project uses those sad orphaned and misshapen wire pieces left behind! Experiment fearlessly—this project is the place to practice all kinds of wireworking techniques.

waste-not bracelet

linda gettings

TECHNIQUES USED

hammering, page 15

simple loops, page 15

coiling, page 18

spiraling, page 18

making jump rings, page 19

s-hooks, page 22

MATERIALS

Leftover pieces of wire at least 1" (2.5 cm) long

Silver, brass, or colored 16-gauge wire

Silver, brass, or colored 18-gauge wire

35–40 gold round beads with holes large enough to
    accommodate the wire

TOOLS

Various-size dowels

Flush cutters

Round-nose pliers

2 chain-nose pliers

Ball-peen hammer

Steel bench block

FINISHED SIZE

8¼" (21 cm)

1. Wind 16g and 18g wire around the various dowels and cut the coils into jump rings.

2. Make a jump ring chain long enough to fit comfortably around your wrist, alternating single and double links. Make a simple hook for closure and attach to the end of the chain.

3. Hold one end of a scrap piece of wire with chain-nose pliers, place it on the bench block, and tap it several times with the hammer. Make a few bends in the wire with round-nose pliers and attach it to the chain with a simple loop.

4. Coil a scrap piece of wire a few times around a dowel. Remove it from the dowel and pull it to make a spring shape. Attach it to the chain with a simple loop.

5. Make a simple loop on one end of a 2" (5 cm) piece of wire. String a few beads and attach it to the chain with a simple loop on the other end.

6. Make a spiral on one end of a piece of wire, make a simple loop, and attach it to the bracelet.

7. Repeat Steps 2–6 to cover the chain as desired.

Here's a fun way to use one of those wonderful stone donuts. Add some beads and charms as dangles and make it into a beautiful pendant that you can hang from a chain or silk or rubber cording.

swingin' style
tamara l. honaman

TECHNIQUES USED
hammering, page 15
simple loops, page 15
spiraling, page 18
coiling, page 18

MATERIALS

16" (40.5 cm) of sterling silver 16-gauge half-hard wire
1 turquoise 45mm donut
1 sterling silver 20-gauge 4mm jump ring
2 sterling silver 16-gauge 5mm jump rings
1 sterling silver 16-gauge 8mm jump ring
1 oval charm
1 Bali silver large snowflake charm
1 turquoise 3mm bead
2 amethyst 6 x 10mm center-drilled teardrop crystals
4 sterling silver 2.5mm round beads
2 Bali silver 4mm daisy spacers
3 sterling silver 1½" (3.8 cm) 24-gauge head pins
18½" (47 cm) rubber cord necklace

TOOLS

Heavy-duty wire cutters
Round-nose pliers
Flat-nose pliers
Ball-peen hammer
Steel bench block

FINISHED SIZE

3½" (9 cm) pendant

1. Cut an 11" (28 cm) length of 16g wire. Flush cut both ends.

2. Place the end of the wire onto the steel bench block. Hammer ¼-½" (6-13 mm) at each end. Turn a small simple loop on one end, then enlarge it with your flat-nose pliers into a spiral slightly wider than the opening of the donut. Measure the remaining wire and subtract from the original 11" (28 cm) to see how much has been used so far.

3. Place the spiral over the hole of the donut and bend the wire around the edge to the other side, leaving space between the donut and the wire. Measure from the back hole of the donut to the end of the remaining wire. If necessary, cut it to match the amount of wire used in the first spiral. Turn a second spiral over the back hole of the donut from the end of the wire until the holes of the two spirals meet through the center of the donut.

4. Flush cut both ends of the remaining 5" (12.5 cm) length of wire. Insert the wire through the hole of one spiral, the donut, and the second spiral until the donut is centered on the wire.

5. Bend the wire in half. Make spirals on each end of wire until the spiral reaches just above the top of the donut but not close enough to rub against the donut.

6. Open the 8mm jump ring and slip it through the center of the top two spirals to join them. Close the jump ring.

7. Open one 5mm jump ring, pass it through the loop of wire around the edge of the donut, and close.

8. String 1 daisy spacer, 1 amethyst teardrop, and 1 round silver bead on 1 head pin; finish with a simple loop. Repeat for a second amethyst dangle.

9. String 1 round silver bead, the turquoise bead, and 1 round silver bead on 1 head pin; finish with a simple loop.

10. Open the 4mm jump ring, string the snowflake charm and the simple loops of the 3 dangles, and close. Open the remaining 5mm jump ring and string the oval pendant, 4mm jump ring, and the 5mm jump ring attached to the loop of wire around the edge of the donut.

11. String the pendant on the rubber necklace.

industrial magic
kerry bogert

Creating a necklace that displays the flat sides of disc beads can be a challenge. This unique twist on a basic wire-wrapped loop allows the discs to float around this necklace. Liver of sulfur gives the links a slightly industrial feel.

TECHNIQUES USED
wrapped loops, page 16
oxidizing, page 23

MATERIALS
8–10' (2.4–3 m) of sterling silver 18-gauge dead-soft wire
12–14 multicolored 22–25mm lampworked discs
    (with ⅛" [3 mm] holes)

TOOLS
Flush cutters
Round-nose pliers
Chain-nose pliers
Needle file
Polishing cloth
Liver of sulfur
Rotary tumbler
Stainless steel shot
Polishing cloth

FINISHED SIZE
20¼" (51.5 cm)

1. Links: Cut a 7" (18 cm) piece of wire. With round-nose pliers, form a soft U-shaped bend in the wire 2" (5 cm) from one end.

2. String 1 disc and allow it to settle in the bend. Make a wire-wrapped loop above the disc, wrapping the shorter end around the longer end. Trim excess wire from the shorter piece, but do not cut the longer end.

3. String 1 disc on the long end of the wire and hold it about ½" (1.3 cm) from the wrap. Make another bend around the second disc bead and wrap the remaining tail around the existing wire wrap. Trim any excess and file the ends if necessary.

4. Repeat Steps 1–3 for the desired length, slipping the first bend of each new piece of wire through a disc on the previous link each time. There should be a disc at each end when the piece is finished.

5. Eye: Repeat Steps 1 and 2 at one end of the necklace. Use round-nose pliers to make a wrapped loop with the long end of wire.

6. Clasp: Repeat Steps 1 and 2 at the other end of the necklace. Make another U-shaped bend in the long end ¾" (2 cm) from the wrap. Pinch the bend closed and wrap the remaining length around the existing wire wrap. With round-nose pliers, form the pinched bend into a hook.

7. Oxidize: Dip the finished necklace in liver of sulfur solution. The liver of sulfur solution should be warm, not hot; hot water can cause thermal shock and crack the lampworked beads.

8. Polish the oxidized piece to highlight the wirework, leaving the grooved areas blackened.

9. Work-harden the necklace by tumbling for about 1½ hours in a rotary tumbler with stainless steel shot. Remove the chain from the tumbler, rinse in clear running water, and dry with a terry towel.

geometry
jodi l. bombardier

TECHNIQUES USED
straightening wire, page 14
simple loops, page 15
wrapped loops, page 16
coiling, page 18
spiraling, page 18
opening and closing jump rings, page 19
spiral hooks, page 21

MATERIALS
20–24" (51–61 cm) of sterling silver 16-gauge half-hard
   wire
6–7' (1.8–2.1 m) of sterling silver 26-gauge dead-soft wire
8" (20.5 cm) of sterling silver 20-gauge dead-soft wire
1 coral 1.5 cm focal bead
6–8 white 4mm bicone crystals
8–10 coral chips
1" (2.5 cm) of large cable chain
1 sterling silver 6mm jump ring

TOOLS
Nylon-jaw straightening pliers
Flush cutters
Round-nose pliers
Chain-nose pliers
Ruler
Sharpie marker
Bracelet mandrel (optional)

FINISHED SIZE
6½–7½" (16.5–19 cm)

This bracelet can take on different looks—make it wide or narrow, use different colored wires, or hammer your frame for texture before adding beads. When you've finished this modern bracelet, you're sure to see wire from a new angle.

1. Frame: Cut and straighten 16" (40.5 cm) of 16g wire. Set the wire parallel to a ruler. Center the focal bead at the 8" mark on the ruler and mark a few millimeters outside the ends of the bead on each side. With chain-nose pliers, make 90° bends in the same direction at each mark.

2. Center the focal bead inside the frame and mark the wire a few millimeters beyond the top of the bead. Make 90° angle bends at each mark in opposite directions.

3. Working on one side of the frame, starting from the center bends and moving out to the end, make random 90° angle bends in the wire, considering the sizes of the coral chips (to avoid making large bends for small beads or small bends for large beads). The last bend should be centered on the width of your bracelet. Leave a 1–1½" (2.5–3.8 cm) unbent tail.

4. Repeat Step 3 for the other half of the bracelet, keeping the dimensions of your bends in proportion to the other half. Place the frame on a ruler or straight edge and mark the wire for the last bend in a straight line with the first end. The two ends must line up straight across from each other in order to affix the clasp. Wipe off the marks with a cotton cloth.

5. Lay out the chips and crystals along the frame in the order in which they'll be attached.

If you have a digital camera, take a picture of the frame with the beads laid out for easy reference while wrapping.

6. Cut a comfortable working length of 26g wire (1–3' [30.5–91.5 cm]). Coil it around the focal-bead section of the frame from the top corner of the bend to about halfway down the same side. Clip the tail and use chain-nose pliers to press the end down onto the frame. It is best to wrap the wire around a corner bend for each bead to keep the wire from slipping up and down on the frame.

7. String the focal bead onto the 26g wire and wrap the wire onto the other side of the center of the frame. Wrap up or down the frame, depending on the placement of the next bead.

8. Attach beads to one half of the frame in the same way as for the focal bead. You may slip a bead onto the wire while wrapping the frame to determine its placement on the frame. If you like the placement, continue wrapping the other end of the wire to the next portion of the frame; if not, remove the bead, place a few more wraps on the frame, and check the placement again before wrapping to the next spot on the frame. Continue adding beads until the first half of the bracelet is finished.

9. Repeat Step 8 for the other side, working from the other side of the focal bead to the end.

10. Gently bend down the ends, using a bracelet mandrel or your wrist to shape. Once the bracelet is shaped, make simple loops on each end, one clockwise and one counterclockwise.

11. Make a spiral hook and attach it to one simple loop side of the bracelet with the jump ring.

12. Attach the chain to the other side of the bracelet. Coil the end of a 2" (5 cm) piece of 20g piece of wire, string 1 crystal and 1 chip, and attach it to the last link of the chain with a wrapped loop.

Czech fire-polished beads mirror the colors of beach glass in this pendant. They add variety to the texture, and their many facets reflect color and movement. If you prefer, adapt the design to showcase several beautiful pebbles.

by the beautiful sea

ronna sarvas weltman

TECHNIQUES USED
spiraling, page 18
wrapped loops, page 16

MATERIALS
2 pieces of beach glass
2' (61 cm) of sterling silver 18-gauge dead-soft wire
1 green 14½" (44.5 cm) double-strand Czech glass
   fire-polished bead pre-made necklace

TOOLS
Flush cutters
Round-nose pliers
Chain-nose pliers

FINISHED SIZE
17½" (44.5 cm)

Choose pieces of glass of similar colors and texture but different shapes so the design will be harmonious but have visual interest.

1. Starting with the piece of glass that you wish to hang on the bottom, begin to loop the wire around the glass horizontally and vertically so it is held firmly in place. Each wrap will cross over the previous wire. Leave a "tail" of about 2" (5 cm). Not all of the wraps need to hug the glass.

2. Form a decorative spiral or swirl with the tail. Form a bead cap by coiling wire over the top of the glass.

3. Bend the remaining wire 90° at the top of the coil so that it points straight up. Wrap the wire vertically and horizontally around the second piece of beach glass. Each wrap will cross over the previous wire

4. On the last wrap, pass the wire underneath one or two of the previous wraps to anchor it against the sea glass. Form a wrapped loop at the top of the pendant large enough to string onto the beaded necklace.

5. String the pendant on the beaded necklace.

LEVEL **1**

Here's a simple earring with an Asian flair. Neither simple loops nor soldering is required—just cross your ends and hammer for texture. The oxidized finish gives these an antique feel.

double-crossed
denise peck

MATERIALS
8" (20.5 cm) of sterling silver 16-gauge
    dead-soft wire
2 sterling silver 6mm jump rings
2 sterling silver 4mm jump rings
2 sterling silver ear wires

TOOLS
Flush cutters
Ring mandrel (or any round mandrel)
2 chain-nose pliers
Ball-peen hammer
Steel bench block
Liver of sulfur
Polishing cloth

FINISHED SIZE
1⅞" (4.8 cm)

1. Cut the 16g wire in half.

2. Hold one piece of wire at its center against the ring mandrel and bend both ends around to the other side of the mandrel until they cross each other. Repeat with the other piece. Hammer both hoops flat on the bench block, then use the round end of the hammer to texture the hoops.

3. Close both 6mm jump rings with 2 pairs of chain-nose pliers and hammer them both flat on the bench block. Hammering them will cause them to reopen slightly. Slip the flattened 6mm rings around each hoop right where the ends cross and close them.

4. Close both 4mm jump rings and hammer them both flat. Hammering them will cause them to open slightly.

5. Attach a 4mm ring and an ear wire to each 6mm ring and close the 4mm rings.

6. Oxidize in liver of sulfur, dry, and polish lightly.

Once you can make a nice ring of wire, you can hang just about anything on it. The hoop portion of these earrings is just a ring with two simple loops on the ends turned perpendicular to each other. Easy!

heaps of rings
denise peck

MATERIALS

8" (20.5 cm) of sterling silver 20-gauge
   dead-soft wire
10 enameled 3.5 x 7.5mm rings
2 sterling silver ear wires

TOOLS

Ring mandrel (or any round mandrel)
Flush cutters
Round-nose pliers
2 chain-nose pliers

FINISHED SIZE

1⅝" (4 cm)

1. Cut the 20g wire in half.

2. Hold one piece of wire with the center pressed against the round mandrel. Wrap both ends around to the other side of the mandrel to form a perfect circle with crossed ends. Repeat with the other piece.

3. Where the ends cross, trim the ends, leaving ⅜" (1 cm) on each end.

4. Use round-nose pliers to make a simple loop on each end of the wires. If necessary, use the chain-nose pliers to bend the loops of each wire perpendicular to each other.

5. String 5 rings on 1 hoop. Open the simple loops, connect the ends, and close. Repeat with the second hoop.

6. Add 1 ear wire to a simple loop on each earring.

Coated copper wire is a great way to spice up wirework and add a dash of color. Choose a mixture of complementary colors and a blend of lampworked glass rings. It is guaranteed to amuse any wearer!

ring-a-ling

kerry bogert

TECHNIQUES USED

simple loops, page 15
coiling, page 18
spiraling, page 18
figure-eight links, page 20
simple hooks, page 20

MATERIALS

2' (61 cm) of sterling silver 16-gauge dead-soft wire

6' (1.8 m) of color-coated copper 20-gauge wire, cut in 3 equal lengths

6 multicolored lampworked rings, 2 each with ¾" (2 cm), ½" (1.3 cm), and ³⁄₁₆" (5 mm) holes

TOOLS

Flush cutters

Round-nose pliers

Chain-nose pliers

Needle file

Rotary tumbler

Stainless steel shot

Polishing cloth

FINISHED SIZE

7½" (19 cm)

1. Cut three 4" (10 cm) pieces of 16g wire. File any sharp ends. Cut three 24" (61 cm) pieces of 20g wire.

2. Coil 1 piece of 20g wire around 1 piece of 16g, leaving about ¾" (2 cm) of the 16g bare at each end. Trim any excess 20g wire. Repeat with remaining wires.

3. With round-nose pliers, form a simple loop at each end of the 16g pieces, leaving about ¼" (6 mm) bare wire between the loop and the colored wrapping.

4. With round-nose pliers, grasp the end loop of one 16g link and use your free hand to begin forming the wrapped portion of the link into a corkscrew-like spiral. When half of the wrapped area is spiraled, turn the piece, grasp the other loop on the opposite end, and form a spiral in toward the rest of the link. Repeat with remaining links.

5. With chain-nose pliers, bend the bare loops on the ends of each link out so they are perpendicular to the spiral.

6. Cut four 1½" (3.8 cm) pieces of 16g wire. File any sharp ends.

7. With round-nose pliers, make a figure-eight link with each 1½" (3.8 cm) piece of wire; do not turn one link perpendicular, but leave the link flat. One side should be about the size of the loop in the wire-wrapped links, and the other side should be large enough to hold a glass ring.

8. Lay out the bracelet. The bracelet shown here uses a ¼" (6 mm) hole ring strung on a coiled link, a figure-eight link, a ¾" (2 cm) hole ring, a ½" (1.3 cm) hole ring strung on a figure-eight link, a coiled link, a ½" (1.3 cm) hole ring strung on a figure-eight link, a ¾" (2 cm) hole ring, a figure-eight link, and a ¼" (6 mm) hole ring strung on a coiled link. The large rings hold the smaller ones in place, while the smaller ones spin and move around on the coiled links.

9. Using chain-nose pliers, open the loops of the figure-eight links and assemble the bracelet.

10. Make a simple hook, being sure that the loop that connects the hook to the bracelet is large enough to trap the ¼" (6 mm) glass ring, and attach it one end link. For the other half of the clasp, bend a 2" (5 cm) length of wire as if to make a simple hook, omitting the initial simple loop. Make a loop with one end of the wire held between the fat portions of the round-nose pliers, then continue to spiral for one-half turn to make a large eye. Attach the other end to the last link with a loop large enough to keep the ¼" (6 mm) glass ring on the end link. Tumble the finished piece in a rotary tumbler with stainless steel shot for about 1 hour and clean with a polishing cloth.

LEVEL 1

This very simple choker can be done in silver, gold, or any color wire you choose. It has a fine drape, making it look more complex than it is. Make a chain with fewer links for a matching bracelet.

2 x 2

linda gettings

TECHNIQUES USED

making jump rings, page 19

opening and closing jump rings, page 19

simple hooks, page 20

MATERIALS

11' (3.4 m) of colored 16-gauge wire

TOOLS

7mm round dowel

Flush cutters

Round-nose pliers

2 chain-nose pliers

FINISHED SIZE

16 3/8" (41.5 cm)

1. Wind the wire into coils on the 7mm round dowel, reserving 4 1/2" (11.5 cm). Cut the coils into 168 jump rings.

2. Using 2 chain-nose pliers, close 2 rings. Attach 2 open rings to these 2 closed rings and close them. Repeat until all the rings are used.

3. With the remaining 4 1/2" (11.5 cm), make a simple hook and a slightly larger jump ring and attach one to each end of the chain for the closure.

Here's a pretty connector link for making any bead bracelet; your treasured beads will stand out against the simple trefoil shape of the links. Five or six beads and round-nose pliers are all you need for a lovely piece.

silver clovers
denise peck

MATERIALS
24" (61 cm) of sterling silver 20-gauge half-hard wire
5 multicolored 15mm lampworked coins

TOOLS
Flush cutters
Round-nose pliers

FINISHED SIZE
7¼" (18.5 cm)

1. Cut five 1¼" (3.2 cm) lengths of wire. Make a simple loop at the end of each to form an eye pin. String a bead onto each eye pin and close with another simple loop.

2. Cut six 2" (5 cm) pieces of 20g wire.

3. With round-nose pliers, make a 6mm simple loop on one end of a 2" (5 cm) piece of wire. Mark the round-nose pliers at the point on the jaw where you made the loop to use as a guide to keep all the rest of the loops consistent.

4. Hold the same piece of wire right next to the first loop at the mark on the pliers. Pull the end of the wire around the jaw to make a second loop right next to the first one.

5. Hold the wire right next to the last loop, at the mark on the pliers. Pull the end of the wire around the jaw to make a third loop to sit between the first and second loop in a clover shape.

6. Repeat Steps 3–5 to make 5 more clover lengths.

7. Open the eyes at each end of the bead links and attach a clover link to each end, alternating a clover link and a bead link for the length of the bracelet.

8. Make a simple hook with the remaining wire and attach to one end.

This simple technique turns a variety of beads into a floating cuff in no time at all. Once you have finished one, make a matching necklace or play with different size beads to create a chunkier bracelet and necklace.

suspended
jodi l. bombardier

MATERIALS
11' (3.4 m) of sterling silver 26-gauge dead-soft wire
16 white 6mm side-drilled freshwater pearls
17 turquoise 8–10mm nuggets
1 silver 2cm 3-strand box clasp

TOOLS
Flush cutters
Round-nose pliers
Chain-nose pliers
Low-stick blue masking tape

FINISHED SIZE
7¼" (18.5 cm)

1. Cut ten 13" (33 cm) pieces of 26g wire. Hold two pieces together with chain-nose pliers and twist them to create a segment of twisted wire about 1½" (3.8 cm) long. String 1 pearl onto one of the wires. Pull the second wire around the pearl and twist the wires together again for ½–¾" (1.3–2 cm). String 1 pearl onto the shorter wire, pull the longer wire around the pearl, and twist again for another ½–¾"

(1.3–2 cm). Repeat this sequence for the length of wire, ending with at least 1½" (3.8 cm) of twisted wire.

2. Repeat Step 1, using turquoise nuggets instead of pearls.

3. Repeat Step 1 to create three more additional strands with a mix of turquoise nuggets and pearls, for a total of 5 twisted strands.

4. String 1 strand through one loop of first half of clasp and make a wrapped loop. Repeat to attach a second strand to the same clasp loop as the first strand. String another strand onto the center clasp loop and make a wrapped loop. String the remaining 2 strands onto the last clasp loop and make wrapped loops on each.

5. Interweave the 5 strands randomly until the bracelet is the desired length. If the bracelet is too long, weave the strands more to shorten.

6. Once the desired length is reached, tape the strands together with low-stick blue masking tape to keep them from unweaving as you wrap the ends to the other side of the clasp. Wrap 2 strands to one clasp loop, 1 strand to the middle clasp loop, and 2 strands to the third clasp loop.

Teardrop-shaped earrings aren't all that unusual, but adding a small bead, seemingly suspended in midair between the wires, creates a whole new look! Choose your own favorite beads to showcase in this unique frame.

tears of blue
denise peck

MATERIALS
7" (18 cm) of sterling silver 18-gauge dead-soft wire
6" (15 cm) of sterling silver 26-gauge dead-soft wire
2 round 14mm beads
1 pair sterling silver ear wires

TOOLS
Flush cutters
Round-nose pliers
Ring mandrel
Ball-peen hammer
Steel bench block
Awl

FINISHED SIZE
1⅞" (4.8 cm)

TECHNIQUES USED
hammering, page 15
wrapped loops, page 16
piercing, page 23

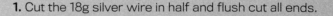

1. Cut the 18g silver wire in half and flush cut all ends.

2. With the wire slightly off-center, bend each piece around the ring mandrel at about size 9 so that one end extends longer than the other. Leave a 14mm space between the two ends to accommodate the round beads.

3. Hammer all the ends flat and use the awl to pierce a hole as close to each end as possible.

4. Cut the 26g wire in half and pass one end through the hole in the shorter end of one teardrop hoop. Wrap to secure.

5. String 1 bead on one 26g wire. Pull the wire taut and pass it through the hole on the long end of the hoop. Bend the wire straight up and make a double wrapped loop for strength. Trim the ends.

6. Repeat Steps 4 and 5 for the second earring.

7. Attach each earring to an ear wire.

LEVEL **1**

jewels of the sea

ronna sarvas weltman

Since no two pieces of beach glass are alike, it's nearly impossible to make a pair of identical earrings. Instead, choose pieces that are similar in color or shape (or both), but vary the wire cages to reflect the planes and angles of each.

MATERIALS
2 small pieces of beach glass
Sterling silver 20-gauge wire
2 sterling silver ear wires

TOOLS
Flush cutters
Round-nose pliers
Chain-nose pliers

FINISHED SIZE
1⁷⁄₈" (4.8 cm)

TECHNIQUES USED
simple loops, page 15

1. Because the earrings are small and the wire wrapping is simple, use the no-waste method: Rather than trying to estimate how much wire you'll need for your earrings, start bending the wire directly from the coil. Make a small free-form squiggle, then use the chain-nose pliers to make a 90° bend in the wire at the top of the squiggle so that the wire points straight up.

2. Wrap the wire vertically around the beach glass, bringing it back down to the bottom so it points straight down, and coil the wire once around the top of the squiggle at the bottom of the beach glass.

3. Continue wrapping diagonally, horizontally, and vertically until the beach glass is held firmly in place and the wire forms an interesting pattern.

4. End at the top of the beach glass by making a few free-form loops. Flush-cut the end and tuck in neatly. Attach an ear wire to the loop.

5. Repeat Steps 1–4 for the second earring.

contributors

KERRY BOGERT is a lampwork bead artist and jewelry designer. She is also a former graphic designer turned stay-at-home

mother of three. To find out more about her unique beads and jewelry, visit kabsconcepts.com or e-mail her at kerry@kabsconcepts.com.

JODI L. BOMBARDIER is a jewelry designer and owner of Jewels by Jules. A self-taught jewelry maker, she

began stringing necklaces in 2002 and later found her niche in wire-wrapped jewelry. Visit her website at jewels-by-jules.com or follow her blog at online-wire-wrapping-instructions.com. She can be reached by e-mail at jodi@jewels-by-jules.com.

LINDA GETTINGS has written over fifty articles for national bead magazines and is currently a contributing editor for *Bead-Patterns*

the Magazine, and her latest patterns can be found at bead-patterns.com. Getting's first book, *Great Beaded Gifts*, was published in 2005. She is

the editor of thedailybeader.com, a monthly newsletter. Reach her by e-mail at ladybeading@aol.com.

TAMARA L. HONAMAN is a jewelry designer who has worked in a variety of media for the past twelve years.

She is the Media Content Manager for Fire Mountain Gems & Beads. The founding editor of *Step by Step Beads*, Honaman frequently contributes jewelry-making projects to books and magazines. She has appeared on PBS's and DIY's *Jewelry Making.*

SANDRA LUPO has been making jewelry for twenty years. She is a wire-jewelry instructor at the Newark Museum Arts Workshop.
Lupo was a contributor to Beading with Crystals, and her work regularly appears in *Step by Step Beads* and *Step by Step Wire Jewelry*. Contact her by e-mail at sandra@sandsstones.com.

DENISE PECK is editor in chief of *Step by Step Wire Jewelry* magazine and senior editor of *Jewelry Artist*. A lifelong lover of jewelry, Denise

went to jewelry-making school in New York City in 1999. She combined her two professions when she joined *Lapidary Journal* in 2004. This is her first book.

HOWARD SIEGEL holds a masters degree in metallurgy and taught at Washington University for ten

years. He has studied at the William Holland School since 1994, where he has taught lost wax casting and advanced chain making since 2000. His chain making articles have appeared in *Art Jewelry*.

RONNA SARVAS WELTMAN has been featured in *Step by Step Wire Jewelry*, *Wire Artist Jeweller*, *Art Jewelry* and Bead Style and

as well as in Easy Beading Volumes 1 and 2. She has been featured on HGTV's *That's Clever!* She lives and teaches jewelry-making techniques in Bellevue, Washington, where she is at work on her first book. Visit her site at ronnaround.com.

sources

SOURCES FOR WIRE
Fire Mountain Gems and Beads
Beads & Beyond
Hauser and Miller
Jatayu
Parawire
Multi Creations Inc.
Munro Crafts
Rio Grande
T.B. Hagstoz
Thunderbird Supply Company

**SOURCES FOR
OTHER MATERIALS**
Daisy Chain Bracelet
Jump Rings: The Ring Lord

All Wrapped Up
Undrilled gem silica and African opal
    beads: Dikra Gem
Chain: Star's Clasps

Definitely Looped
Lampworked glass beads: Kab's
    Creative Concepts

S is for Silver
Charms: Fire Mountain Gems and Beads
Lampworked bead: Lori Copeland,
    Wildfire Designs
Ribbon: Fire Mountain Gems and Beads

I'm Hooked
Leather: Beads & Beyond

Grape Clusters
Freshwater pearls and fluorite semi-
    precious stones: Tucson Gem Center
Bali silver daisy spacers: Holy and Pure
    Gemstones
Sterling silver chain: SII Findings

Glass Nests
Lampworked beads: Family Glass
All other components: Fire Mountain
    Gems and Beads

Winding Vines
Leaf beads: Big Stone
Silver Springs

Bali beads: Nina Designs

Asian Wisdom
Copper chain, silver beads:
    Beads & Beyond
Serpentine pendant: All Seasons Co.
Turquoise: Beads & Beyond

Encrusted Cuff
Freshwater pearls and rose quartz:
    Tucson Gem Center
Bali silver daisy spacers: Holy and Pure
    Gemstones
Swarovski crystal: ABC Direct

So Cagey!
Satin Cording: Fran Lizardi,
    Deepwood Art

Pretty Pulleys
Jump rings: T.B. Hagstoz
London blue topaz briolettes: Stone USA

Exclamation Points
Ear wires and all silver:
    Multi Creations Inc.
Blue glass beads: Michael's

Simply Charming
All materials: Fire Mountain Gems and
    Beads

King of Rings
6mm faceted beads: Michaels
4mm metal beads: Whimbeads

Catch-All
Chain: Beads & Beyond

Rolling Rings
Lampworked glass beads: Kab's
    Creative Concepts

Framed and Coiled
Amazonite nuggets: Tucson Gem Center
Sterling silver chain: SII Findings
Peacock toggle: Rishashay

Coiled Again
Lampworked beads: Lauri Copeland,
    Wildfire-Designs

Twigs
Copper sheet: Jatayu
SoftGlas tubing and connectors:
    The Clay Store

Twisted Bracelet
Clasp: Kamal Trading Company

Elemental
Pink Peruvian opal drilled pendant:
    The Birds and the Beads
Drilled pebbles: Riverstone Bead Co.
Shell pendant: Priscila Marban
Bone ring: Hands of the Hills

French Rope
Clasp: Kamal Trading Company

All That Glitters
Sequins: Michaels

Overwrought
Beads: Taj Company

Grapevine
Freshwater pearls: Tucson Gem Center
Bali silver daisy spacers: Holy and Pure
    Gemstones
Swarovski crystal: ABC Direct

Sticks and Stones
Beads: Blue Santa Beads
Focal bead: beadsbegan
Metal beads: Out on a Whim

Ribbons
Lampworked glass beads: Kab's
    Creative Concepts
Large-hole sterling spacers: Fire
    Mountain Gems and Beads

Finders Keepers
Chain: Beads & Beyond
Hand-dyed silk: Beads & Beyond

Tourmaline Columns
Tourmaline beads: Taj Company

Singular Sensation
Beads: Birds and the Beads

sources

Opal Waves
Peruvian opals: Rincon Trading
Company

Unparalleled
Clasp: Kamal Trading Company

Waste Not Bracelet
Beads: My Father's Beads

Swingin' Style
All components: Fire Mountain
Gems and Beads

Industrial Magic
Lampworked glass beads:
Kab's Creative Concepts

Geometry
Coral: DAH Rock Shop
Swarovski crystal: ABC Direct
Chain: SII Findings

By the Beautiful Sea
Glass beads: Beads & Beyond

Heaps of Rings
Enameled rings: Michaels

Ring-a-Ling
Lampworked glass beads:
Kab's Creative Concepts

Silver Clovers
Lampworked beads: Grace Beads

Suspended
Freshwater pearls and turquoise:
Tucson Gem Center
Clasp: Rishashay

Tears of Blue
Ear wires: Multi Creations Inc.
Beads: Nguni Imports

**CONTACT
INFORMATION**

ABC Direct
349 E. Ft. Lowell
Tucson, AZ 85705
(877) 696-9490
abcdirectbeads.com

All Seasons Company
888 Brannan St., #1160
San Francisco, CA 94103
(800) 700-5233
allseason.com

Beads & Beyond
25 102nd Ave. NE
Bellevue, WA 98004-5676
(425) 462-8992
beadsandbeyond-wa.com

Big Stone Beads & Findings
6222 Richmond Ave., Ste. 401
Houston, TX 77057
(713) 783-1855

The Birds and the Beads
411 Route 79
Morganville, NJ 07751-9772
(732) 591-8233
thebirdsandthebeads.com

Blue Santa Beads
18 North Pennell Rd.
Media, PA 19063
(610) 892-2740
bluesanta-beads.com

The Clay Store
(877) 602-0700
theclaystore.com

DAH Rock Shop
3401 North Dodge Blvd.
Tucson, AZ 85716
(520) 323-0781

Deepwood Art
Fran Lizardi
deepwoodart.com

Dikra Gem
56 West 45th St.
New York, NY 10036
(800) 873-4572
dikragem.net

Family Glass
(913) 231-1313
familyglass.com

Fire Mountain Gems and Beads
One Fire Mountain Wy.
Grants Pass, OR 97526-2373
(800) 355-2137
firemountaingems.com

**Grace Lampwork
Beads and Jewelry Inc.**
PO Box 360468
Milpitas, CA 95036
(408) 526-9700
gracebeads.com

Hauser & Miller Co.
10950 Lin-Valle Dr.
St. Louis, MO 63123
(800) 462-7447
hauserandmiller.com

Holy and Pure Gemstones
254-15 Northern Blvd.
Little Neck, NY 11362
(718) 225-6850
holygemstone.com

Jatayu
Connie Fox
(888) 350-6481
conniefox.com

Kab's Creative Concepts
Kerry Bogert
5799 Coppersmith Trail
Ontario, NY 14519
(585) 944-0141
kabsconcepts.com

Kamal Trading Company
2622 W. Lincoln Ave., #101
Anaheim, CA 92801
(800) 260-0567
kamaltrading.com

Michaels Stores
michaels.com

Multi Creations Inc.
(732) 607-6422
multicreationsnj.com

Munro Crafts
3954 12 Mile Rd.
Berkley, MI 48072
(248) 544-1590
munrocrafts.com

My Father's Beads
702 West State St.
Coopersburg, PA 18036
(610) 282-6939
myfathersbeads.com

Nina Designs
PO Box 8127
Emeryville, CA 94662
(800) 336-6462
ninadesigns.com

Nguni Imports
PO Box 807
Irmo, SC 29063
(803) 407-1601
nguni.com

Out on a Whim
121 E. Cotati Ave.
Cotati, CA 94931
(800) 232-3111
whimbeads.com

Parawire
2-8 Central Ave.
East Orange, NJ 07018
(973) 672-0500
parawire.com

The Ring Lord
290C RR6
Saskatoon SK
Canada S7K 3J9
(306) 374-1335
theringlord.com

Rio Grande
7500 Bluewater Rd. NW
Albuquerque, NM 87121-1962
(800) 545-6566
riogrande.com

Rincon Trading Company
PO Box 69208
Tucson, AZ 85737
(520) 219-3058
rincontradingcompany.com

Rishashay
PO Box 8271
Missoula, MT 59807
(800) 517-3311
rishashay.com

SII Findings
(866) 434-6346
siifindings.com

Star's Clasps
139A Church St., N.W.
Vienna, VA 22180
(800) 207-2807
starsclasps.com

Stone USA Inc.
1170 Broadway, Ste. 1011-1014
New York, NY 10001
(212) 447-5268

Taj Company
42 West 48th St.
14th Fl.
New York, NY 10036
(800) 325-0825
tajcompany.com

T.B. Hagstoz
709 Sanson St.
Philadelphia, PA 19106
(800) 922-1006
hagstoz.com

Thunderbird Supply Company
1907 W. Historic Route 66
Gallup, NM 87301
(800) 545-7968
thunderbirdsupply.com

Tucson Gem Center
234 W Plata St.
Tucson, AZ 85705
(520) 495-4076
tucsongemcenter.com

Wildfire-Designs
Lauri Copeland
wildfire-designs.com

further reading

BOOKS

Chandler, Linda and Christine Ritchey. *Woven Wire Jewelry: Contemporary Designs and Creative Techniques.* Loveland, Colorado: Interweave, 2004.

Jones, Linda. *Making Colorful Wire and Beaded Jewelry: 35 Fabulous Designs.* Loveland, Colorado: Interweave, 2006.

Jones, Liz. *Jewelry Studio: Silver Wire Fusing.* Loveland, Colorado: Interweave, 2008.

Lareau, Mark. *Getting Started Making Metal Jewelry.* Loveland, Colorado: Interweave, 2007.

Wiseman, Nancie. *Crochet with Wire.* Loveland, Colorado: Interweave, 2005.

——— *Knitting with Wire.* Loveland, Colorado: Interweave, 2003.

MAGAZINES

Beadwork
Jewelry Artist
Step by Step Wire Jewelry
Stringing

index

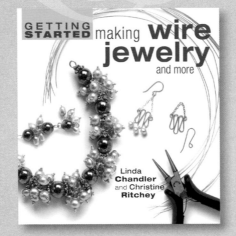
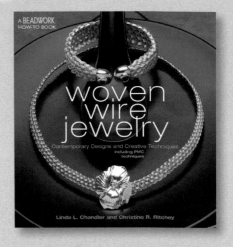
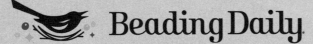